ECOLOGIST

guide to Food

Andrew Wasley

Leaping Hare Press

First published in the UK in 2014 by

Leaping Hare Press

210 High Street, Lewes
East Sussex BN7 2NS, UK
www.leapingharepress.co.uk

British Library Cataloguing-in-Publication Data
A catalogue record for this book is available from
the British Library

ISBN: 978-1-78240-054-7
This book was conceived, designed and produced by

Leaping Hare Press

Creative Director PETER BRIDGEWATER
Publisher SUSAN KELLY
Commissioning Editor MONICA PERDONI
Art Director JAMES LAWRENCE
Senior Editors JACQUI SAYERS & JAYNE ANSELL
Designer GINNY ZEAL
Illustrator LUCY KIRK

Printed sustainably by
TJ International Ltd, Padstow, Cornwall, UK
using FSC® certified paper and vegetable based inks
Colour Origination by Ivy Press Reprographics

Distributed worldwide (except North America) by
Thames & Hudson Ltd., 181A High Holborn,
London WC1V 7QX, United Kingdom

1 3 5 7 9 10 8 6 4 2

CONTENTS

FOREWORD

The Ecologist has been setting the environmental agenda for over 40 years – bringing the critical issues of our time into the mainstream through cutting-edge reporting, as well as pioneering original thinking and inspiring action. Whether it's challenging vast corporations, exposing corruption or shining a light on unquestioned orthodoxies, *The Ecologist* remains to this day the world's leading environmental affairs title.

As the environmental debate has evolved and increasingly moved into the mainstream, *The Ecologist* has placed more emphasis on promoting ethical consumerism. This has included the publication of practical green living advice, as well as reportage around the issues concerning our day to day products and lifestyle choices.

Perhaps most well known is the critically-acclaimed Behind The Label (BTL) series, in which health commentator and ex-*Ecologist* editor Pat Thomas deconstructed the ingredients of some of our most popular and seemingly innocent products. From unearthing the chemical nasties in your body cream and revealing what's really in your bottle of tomato ketchup to examining the devastation your 'dolphin-friendly' tuna might actually be causing, this column has been scrutinizing the contents of the nation's shopping baskets for more than 8 years.

More recently, the series evolved into Behind The Brand (BTB), which took readers on a whistle-stop tour to the heart of some of the world's largest corporations. From Bernard Matthews to IKEA, the BTB columns investigated the claims made against the companies in question, and examined the 'greenwash' effect, questioning whether some companies truly were 'green'.

Elsewhere, *The Ecologist* has repeatedly exposed the 'hidden costs' of many consumerables. From palm oil to petrol, tinned tomatoes to timber, bananas to beef, its unique investigations, some of them undercover and carried out at great personal risk, have taken readers on a unique journey to some of the world's environmental front lines to bring back the often unpalatable truths about many of the consumer goods we take for granted. In recent years the intrepid Ecologist Film Unit has trod where few others have dared to go and shone a much needed spotlight on some of the world's most unreported environmental issues.

Building on all of this, *The Ecologist* is producing the much anticipated *Ecologist Guides*. Drawing from the magazine's unique archive, and containing much new material, the series will be written by leading experts in the field and will cover a range of topics on the environmental agenda, presenting the often hard truths surrounding these themes, and offering enlightening debate as they consider the changes that need to be made. The guides – sometimes surprising, sometimes controversial – will be essential reading for anyone interested in making ethical choices and living a more sustainable life.

Zac Goldsmith
Environmental Campaigner, MP
and Editor of The Ecologist, 1998–2007

INTRODUCTION

THE HIDDEN COST OF CHOICE If you are reading this, you are probably lucky enough to live in the 'developed' world, where – as long as you have the means of paying for it – there are seemingly endless food choices and a year-round abundance of often frighteningly cheap foodstuffs from every corner of the earth.

This choice is available only as the result of an increasingly industrialized farming and food production system. One that comes with a 'hidden' price tag – from often cruel and barbaric farming methods to the decline in small, traditional farms, a loss of community, human rights abuses, the destruction of ecosystems and loss of biodiversity, pollution and waste, the spread of disease, an unsustainable reliance on fossil fuels... the list is endless.

Add to this the 'bigger' challenges facing the planet – climate change, a rising population, water shortages – and you have a potential recipe for disaster. Quite simply, our current food system cannot continue as it is.

For over 40 years, *The Ecologist* magazine has been covering food in a way few others could (or would) – investigating unpalatable truths, going against the grain, delving behind the labels (literally), uncovering scandals, reporting on seemingly distant problems, championing maverick thinking ahead of its time, as well as giving a voice to some of those marginalized in more mainstream debates.

As a journalist and undercover investigator specializing in food issues, I've been able to see, often at first hand, just how broken our food system has become. My reporting has enabled me to shine a light on some of the murkier corners of the global food industry. The bits they don't want you to read about. The bits that get glossed over on the labels and in the slick advertising. The bits, quite frankly, that would put you off your food and – in more cases than one – the bits that could (and would) make you ill.

It's been a disturbing journey, but also an inspiring one, and I've been lucky enough to meet some of the growing number of pioneering (and sometimes brave) individuals – farmers, producers, activists and others – challenging the status quo and showing there are humane, sustainable and viable alternatives.

This book draws together some of these findings. Some have been published before, either in *The Ecologist* or elsewhere; others are new or appearing for the first time. The book also highlights some of the magazine's most original food reporting from recent years. Some of the pieces are effectively cut-down snapshots of much longer *Ecologist* reports, designed to offer readers a taste of particular issues around certain foodstuffs. Others – particularly where the original reporting was highly powerful or groundbreaking

– make use of much longer excerpts, and point readers towards potential solutions to the issues.

This book is not a shopping guide. Or a food guide in a traditional sense, where an A to Z of foodstuffs are profiled and given an ethical rating – there are plenty of those already. And it doesn't pretend to be comprehensive: to cover all the issues connected to our modern food system we'd need a book many times the size of this one. No, this book serves to highlight some of the surprising truths about what we put into our mouths each day – where it comes from, at what cost and what the alternatives might be.

1 Fruit

INTRODUCTION

Recent years have brought a crop of headlines highlighting disturbing problems connected to our love affair with fruit. Tropical fruit grown in developing countries has generated some of the most serious concerns, with the alarm being raised over food miles and packaging, health and pesticide use, unfair trade mechanisms, the power of supermarkets, as well as conditions for workers toiling in the plantations and packhouses.

The Ecologist has been at the forefront of this reporting, investigating the complex supply chains that keep our supermarket shelves stuffed, and examining the often uneven economics of production that perpetuate poverty and suffering, rather than address it. Some of these reports are highlighted here, where we also ask whether ethical certification schemes really live up to the hype, talk to campaigners about successes in cleaning up the pineapple trade and highlight some of the bold producers selling fruit in a more sustainable and inspiring fashion.

THE DEADLY LEGACY OF GUATEMALA'S BANANA TRADE

Life for many people employed on the central American country's vast banana plantations is miserable, with low wages, poor living conditions and little access to healthcare. But trade unions trying to secure a better deal for the banana workers face the daily threat of violence and death as powerful interests seek to thwart them.

Assassinations

Standing up for the rights of workers, rural communities and indigenous people in Guatemala can be a deadly business. The International Trade Union Federation (ITUC) says that ten activists were killed in 2011 alone, all brutally

assassinated in the course of their work trying to help others fight off exploitation, marginalization or other threats.

Six of those murdered were connected to the country's Izabal Banana Workers' Union (SITRABI) – which defends some of those toiling in the plantations that make up the country's vast banana industry. At least ten SITRABI activists have been killed since 2007, grim statistics that serve to make Guatemala officially the second most dangerous country in the world, after Colombia, in which to be a trade unionist.

Guatemala's banana sector has mushroomed in recent years, and is now responsible for exporting nearly 10 per cent of the world's bananas – an estimated 1.3–1.4 million tonnes of fruit per annum. The US is the main destination for Guatemalan bananas, and the leading purchaser of the country's crop. But how many American consumers are aware that their fruit could be linked to such a bloody chain of violence?

Corruption

'On May 26 [2011], Idar Joel Hernandez Godoy left his home and drove towards the headquarters of SITRABI in the town of Morales,' a briefing by the Make Fruit Fair campaign reports. 'It was about 7:20am when two men on a motorcycle

intercepted him as he was crossing the small village of Christina. Idar Joel was killed by four bullets in the head and one in the shoulder. […] Idar Joel, 50, leaves three orphaned daughters.'

Activists say such killings highlight the corruption and culture of impunity that persists across Guatemala. Idar's murder prompted Amnesty International to intervene, calling on the authorities to investigate the crime and to take urgent steps to better protect trade unionists.

Much of Guatemala's banana production is centred around two areas – the 'Pacific south' and the Caribbean zone around Izabal. Conditions have improved significantly in recent years for many of those employed in the Caribbean zone. However, in the south, following the unionization of workers at all major plantations and ongoing dialogue between producers and workers' representatives, the situation remains 'harsh', activists say.

A COMPLEX REALITY

The problem with attributing responsibility for the continuing toll of trade union and social movement activist murders in Guatemala is that they take place in the context of a very high murder rate for all sectors of society, including business-men, writes Jacqui Mackay of Banana Link.

The fact that the murders take place in a country with almost total impunity makes it even harder. Unless the fruit companies muster the political will to use their considerable influence to leverage proper judicial procedures concerning crimes committed against their employees, it is hard to see the situation improving.

WANT MORE INFO?
www.makefruitfair.org.uk

HOW FAIR ARE ORGANIC & FAIRTRADE BANANAS?

Bananas are one of the world's favourite foods – globally, consumers spend in excess of $10billion on the fruit every year. They are also one of the world's most important crops – behind only maize, rice and wheat – for helping to maintain food security in developing countries.

Price war

But banana farming has been linked to a host of serious environmental problems, including deforestation, pesticide use and water contamination, as well as poor working and living conditions for farmworkers, some of whom toil for the equivalent of just £1 a day.

In the UK, a particularly bitter banana 'price war' between rival supermarkets put pressure on growers to produce the fruit as cheaply as possible. But there has also been a drive in recent years to grow more bananas to organic and Fairtrade standards, to help guarantee better environmental practices and a better deal for workers.

Several major supermarkets have committed to sourcing all their bananas from Fairtrade suppliers, creating a UK market worth £208 million in 2011.

'Barely enough to eat'

While this has undoubtedly improved standards, in the Dominican Republic – a major supplier of organic and Fairtrade bananas – the picture is more complex, as *The Ecologist*'s former deputy editor Tom Levitt uncovered. Although some of the health and environmental problems associated with conventional banana growing were not apparent, he found squalid conditions and low pay for many plantation workers – chiefly undocumented migrants from Haiti: 'Lying hidden off a main road, around 1,000 Haitian migrants live crowded together in a community of corrugated iron shacks. Most of them are young and male, some have families

> **Most of the workers get 250 to 300 pesos a day when they work (about £4). "It is barely enough to eat ... It allows us one meal a day of beans and rice ..."**

but no one has water, toilets or electricity. [...] Of the ones that do [have jobs], nearly all work on banana plantations, including some for a well-known organic plantation. Most of the workers get 250 to 300 pesos a day when they work (about £4). "It is barely enough to eat," a group of young men tell us. "It allows us one meal a day of beans and rice but is not enough to rent a house or look after a family."

In response, the Fairtrade Foundation said it was working to resolve the problem, but action by the authorities was needed to grant the migrants residency status and allow them access to social security. Undocumented workers have no status or bargaining power, and are therefore vulnerable to exploitative practices.

THE WORKERS' STORIES

Jan Luis Moneta migrated from Haiti, one of the poorest countries in the world, when he was 14 years old. After 30 years working on banana plantations he is still classed as an illegal worker. With his daily wage he cannot afford to live in anything more than a corrugated iron hut, with no water, toilet facilities or electricity.

Emmantel Audige is employed on a Fairtrade-certified banana plantation. He told us that he and other migrants had signed a contract for eight hours a day but actually worked 6am to 5pm without rest or overtime, for wages of no more than the average 250 pesos reported by non-Fairtrade workers. He said he had been in the country for 11 years but was still an illegal worker, with no rights to social security.

WANT MORE INFO?

www.bananalink.org.uk
www.fairtrade.org.uk
www.consumersinternational.org

CLEANING UP THE PINEAPPLE CHAIN

This tropical fruit has long been associated with appalling labour practices and environmental damage linked to intensively farmed plantations. But a sustained international campaign is trying to change all that for good. *The Ecologist* talked with **Jacqui Mackay**, BANANA LINK's campaign coordinator, to find out just how much progress has been made and what obstacles remain.

Ecologist: *Many consumers won't be fully aware of the extent of the problems traditionally connected to the pineapple trade. What are the main issues – both concerning workers' rights and environmental impacts – that have tarnished the fruit's image?*

> **Many plantations and packing plants operate 24 hours a day – at night, workers struggle to see without adequate lighting and snakes have caused a number of deaths.**

Jacqui Mackay: Seventy-five per cent of internationally traded pineapples come from Costa Rica, where low wages are estimated to be half of what is needed to live on. Workers therefore have to work up to 80 hours a week to survive. Working conditions are awful with workers directly exposed to sun and heavy rains without shelter, even during breaks. Heavy and repetitive tasks put enormous strain on workers' health. Many plantations and packing plants operate 24 hours a day – at night, workers struggle to see without adequate lighting and snakes have caused a number of deaths.

Exposure to toxic agrochemicals causes problems from skin and eye irritations, birth defects and male sterility, and psychological problems such as anxiety and depression.

Seventy per cent of workers are Nicaraguan migrants, often without official papers or visas, leaving them particularly vulnerable to the power of employers […]. These migrant workers are the 'secret' of Costa Rica's pineapple success story. Poor environmental practices cause problems – the contamination of ground water, soil erosion and deforestation. Some communities in the South Atlantic zone now have drinking water brought in by government tankers because toxic chemicals from pineapple production have polluted the local supply.

Ecologist: *Recently there's been a big drive to 'clean up' the pineapple chain in certain countries – could you outline the background to that and tell us what steps have been taken to improve things?*

JM: Costa Rican unions and environmental campaigners have been working hard for many years to improve conditions in the industry but a big impetus came from research commissioned by Consumers International in 2010 into the Costa Rican industry. [This] exposed how value is distributed along the pineapple supply chain – workers receiving 4 per cent and retailers 41 per cent – as well as the serious social and environmental impacts of this export production. Media coverage triggered questions being asked in the Costa Rican Parliament and caused widespread industry debate.

> **Some communities in the South Atlantic zone now have drinking water brought in by government tankers because toxic chemicals from pineapple production have polluted the local supply.**

RESPONSIBLE PINEAPPLE PRODUCTION

In June 2011 the United Nations Development Programme (UNDP) convened the National Platform of Responsible Production and Trade of Costa Rican Pineapple. The platform began with an environmental focus but years of conflict and distrust are hard to overcome and affected communities and environmental NGOs have called the platform a 'green disguise' to protect pineapple exports. In February 2013, some environmental NGOs and unions issued press releases denouncing the platform.

Ecologist: *What real benefits will this have brought to those working down the chain – are there examples of lives actually being changed?*

JM: Sadly, union leaders report that conditions in 2013 are no better than when the research was conducted, in fact the situation worsens as living costs rise. However, although unions see the National Platform as a failure, they are still keen to engage in dialogue with industry and government, and have called on the Labour Ministry to talk with the unions involved and start addressing some of the basic problems facing workers outside the platform.

One of our union partners, SITRAP, has proposed a big gathering of the social and environmental organizations to work out where the campaign to create a more sustainable industry can go from here. Consumers can support this work and show solidarity with our union partners by donating to our Union to Union programme. This builds the capacity of unions to organize, educate and advocate on behalf of the workers who remain in poverty and are exposed daily to the harsh conditions of pineapple production.

> **Everyone in the supply chain – from producer to consumer – has a responsibility and a role to play in ensuring fruit is produced ethically and sustainably.**

Ecologist: *Whose responsibility ultimately is it to ensure pineapples – and indeed other fruit – on sale in supermarkets and used as ingredients in processed food really are produced ethically and sustainably?*

JM: Everyone in the supply chain – from producer to consumer – has a responsibility and a role to play in ensuring fruit is produced ethically and sustainably. However, the power to do this differs enormously and this is the crux of the problem. Those with the most power arguably have the most responsibility and in the case of pineapples, as with other foodstuffs, this is the supermarkets.

Putting pressure on supermarkets – many of whom are increasingly sourcing directly from plantations – to improve their voluntary standards is one approach, but ultimately our goal is the regulation of supermarket buyer power.

> ... if we all stopped buying pineapples tomorrow, what would happen to the thousands of workers whose livelihoods are dependent upon this export trade?

THE SUPERMARKET 'BOTTLENECK'

The concentration of power along supply chains in the hands of supermarkets is often described as a 'bottleneck'; there are millions of consumers [in the UK] and our food is grown by millions of farmers/producers, but only a handful of retailers act as gatekeepers controlling this supply. Supermarkets abuse the buyer power this gives them, resulting in downward pressure on prices that squeeze the most flexible cost in the chain: labour. The increasing pressure of low retail prices further decreases the capacity of producers to invest in the improvement of conditions on their plantations.

Ecologist: *There's clearly been some progress in tackling the problems associated with pineapples, but isn't the simple answer to encourage consumers not to buy, or to buy less, fruit sourced overseas and prioritize domestic, seasonal foodstuffs?*

JM: Is there ever a simple answer? For consumers, the choice of where to source fruit from is a personal one. […] In the long term, choosing local produce over tropical fruit is the more sustainable answer – however, if we all stopped buying pineapples tomorrow, what would happen to the thousands of workers whose livelihoods are dependent upon this export trade? […] If we choose local seasonal products, then we have to consider how we can responsibly support communities to reduce their dependency on the livelihoods provided by export trades and focus on producing foods for local markets.

WANT MORE INFO?
www.bananalink.org.uk/
why-pineapples-matter

THE PERUVIAN MANGO TRADE

According to research by the Dutch group SOMO, our taste for tropical fruit is fuelling poor conditions for some of those working down the supply chain – but Peru's vast mango industry maintains it is providing jobs and improving stability where little existed before.

The export curse?

Mangoes are grown in a number of different countries, including South Africa, Brazil, Ecuador, Costa Rica and Peru. Some of the largest markets for mangoes include the US and Western European countries.

Peru's mango industry is largely export-orientated, with some 300,000 tonnes of the fruit estimated to be harvested and sent overseas each year, much of it destined for European supermarkets. However, Peru's mango producers have come under fire after a number of allegations of substandard conditions in the supply chain were made by researchers from the Dutch organization, the Centre for Research on Multinational Corporations (SOMO).

SOMO examined conditions for workers connected to three large Peruvian companies trading in mangoes, two of them supplying a number of well-known European supermarkets. The group says that during its inquiry – the first of its kind in Peru – it uncovered a number of disturbingly exploitative practices and problems, including poverty wages, excessive working hours, unpaid – and forced – overtime, unsatisfactory contractual arrangements, poor health and safety practices, and discrimination against pregnant women and those organizing themselves or others into unions.

Claims are from another era

But the allegations have been strongly refuted by the companies involved. *The Ecologist* reporter Gervase Poulden, sent to follow up independently on the SOMO research, was told by one company that it had actually brought formality, improved conditions and secure jobs to areas where none existed previously.

'I think a lot of these people [workers interviewed by SOMO] are thinking and talking about older concepts and habits,' the company's corporate affairs manager told Poulden. 'This company as it is today was formed in 2008, before that it was the property of another family.

Perhaps before they had this type of behaviour.'

The company also disputed that by paying the industry standard to workers – in most cases the Peruvian minimum wage (about £175 per month), regarded by SOMO as a poverty wage – it was doing anything wrong: 'People say, "but these workers gain the minimum wage". Well, before that they earned nothing, or they were working informally, without any protection from the state.'

WANT MORE INFO?
www.somo.nl

VOICES FROM THE HARVEST

Octavia, mango collector
'Although I work the whole year, I have signed a contract for three or four months only. I get to sign such a temporary contract once a year. For a two-week period I get about 280 PEN (100 USD). In the pay slips they sometimes give me, my extra hours are noted but sometimes they are not.'

Juan, fieldworker
'In 2005, I worked in harvesting and we didn't have piece-rates, we had to work a certain number of hours a day. The piece-rates came in later, and the supervisors are constantly elevating the targets, now they ask for 90 boxes a pair. If we do our job fast, they might even raise our target again up to 120 boxes a day. We are never able to reach the target in eight hours and they are not paying us for this overtime. In harvest season I start working at 6am and finish at 7pm.

A TALE OF TWO APPLE FARMS

The organic movement faces a dilemma. Should it remain true to its roots and stick with local, informal production methods and distribution, shunning the despised supermarkets? Or should it embrace technology and seek to feed as many mouths as possible?

Computer-assisted growing

Sitting in front of his computer in a neat office in a smart farmhouse in the village of Marden in Kent, Peter Hall talks me through his modern, high-tech approach to apple farming. The talk is of maximizing outputs, increasing yields, and disease and crop management, as well as how to meet the standards required by supermarkets. It's complex and impressive stuff, especially the computer programmes that help with predicting plant diseases, and the sophisticated weather station that enables better planning of cultivation and harvesting.

Peter manages HE Hall & Son, an established fruit farming business that has been around since the nineteenth century and today sees the growing and selling of significant quantities of apples and pears, hops and other crops from just over 100 hectares

of Kent countryside. Much of the land is farmed using conventional techniques – albeit with an emphasis on sustainability – with the remainder certified as organic by the Soil Association.

The company is a supplier to a large supermarket chain and is working with the retailer to develop and fine-tune its organic fruit-growing techniques, including designing crop protection systems that – it is hoped – will be able to be adopted by conventional growers.

Intensive-organic

In contrast to the commonly perceived image of organic production (traditional, old-fashioned, get-your-hands-dirty stuff, with muddy fruit and vegetables delivered in a transit van), the operation here is slick with a businesslike approach embracing scientific research. This is 'intensive-organic' farming, with the emphasis on producing as much as possible in the least environmentally damaging way. And on making some money along the way. You suspect the fruit from here is shiny and clean-looking.

But for some traditionalists in the organic movement – both growers and consumers – supplying the supermarkets, or multiples as they are known in the trade, remains akin to doing business with the devil. It is seen as feeding the modern, industrial agribusiness system that's so often blamed for decimating traditional food culture and locally focused supply chains. Supply, or buy, from these retail beasts and you are contributing to the problem, so the argument goes.

Others want to do business with the supermarkets – often on economic grounds – but say that the unfair rules of the game keep them out of the club; if the approach, scale and product are not absolutely perfect, they argue, they'll reject you out of hand.

Upscaling organics

Peter is pragmatic and convinced his approach is where the future lies: 'You don't have to have a Luddite approach, just because it's old doesn't mean it's good,' he says. 'We're growing organically using science and technology… cherry picking the best bits.'

Citing the big environmental problems facing the country (and indeed the world), particularly climate change, he argues that upscaled organic and sustainable production offers a way of tackling these issues. 'It is about industrializing the process so [we can] bring organic food to more people,' he says. 'It has a [knock on] impact and influence on the conventional sector, [and shows] an efficient use of source resources.'

He's sympathetic – and deeply respectful – of smaller scale producers, including those who complain about the approach of supermarkets, or those struggling to access the market. But he says some simply do not realize what it involves: 'If you want to do business with the multiples, it's [a] 24/7 operation … seven days a week to get it done, to make it work…. Supermarkets are not interested in [selling a product] for two weeks.'

… [this] modern, high-tech approach to apple farming [is] complex and impressive stuff, especially the computer programmes that help with predicting plant diseases, and the sophisticated weather station that enables better planning of cultivation and harvesting.

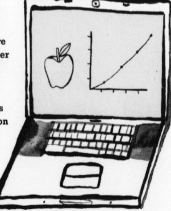

Keeping it small (& local)

One producer with a different view is Matthew Wilson, who, with his wife Carol, runs the organic Oakwood Farm orchard in Robertsbridge, Sussex, which supplies apples, juice and cider to restaurants, pubs and hotels, and direct to the public via farmers' markets and other similar 'direct' routes.

They are critical of some supermarkets' treatment of suppliers and believe that the 'organic ethic' should permeate every aspect of their business. 'We like the personal touch, we like to speak to people [customers] directly; that's always been the main part of our business,' says Matthew. 'There's no substitute for getting out there and meeting people.'

Oakwood's approach is probably closer to the traditional image of organic production and supply that most people have – the company doesn't even have its own website or online shop. And Matthew believes that the supermarkets haven't got it right on everything, including their apparent obsession with presentation.

He says that, in his experience, customers are not overly worried whether their fruit has blemishes, comes in odd shapes or looks less than polished: 'At farmers' markets, we grade for quality, not size. People want variety – colours, shapes, sizes – they don't mind what they get.'

As the principal organic certifier in the UK, we asked the SOIL ASSOCIATION's **Tom MacMillan** how it views the apparent tensions that arise from the upscaling of organic production.

Ecologist: *Does the SA believe it is possible for the true ethos of sustainable, organic (fruit) production to be retained when growers become suppliers to the large multiples?*

Tom MacMillan: Producers like Peter Hall show it is possible to scale up organic fruit production and still adhere to organic principles – it gets more complicated the bigger a farm gets, but good farm management is the key. This issue comes up particularly in fruit production because it is not easy to grow some fruit well in many parts of the UK, so a lot gets grown at a fairly large scale in the south-east, Herefordshire and Somerset, then transported around the country.

Although many organic farmers run small- to medium-sized, mixed systems, organic standards don't specify what size a farm has to be; just what standards they have to adhere to and what inputs they are allowed to use. Lorries can be a relatively efficient way of transporting fruit compared to lots of little vans, though growers should perhaps be looking at breeding varieties that require less chilled storage and keep better in ambient temperatures.

Ecologist: *To what extent does the SA believe that the future expansion of the organic sector can only be successful by increased trade with the large multiples?*

TM: Around three-quarters of organic food is bought through supermarkets. We want to make sure that farmers and shoppers who sell and buy food that way get a fair deal, so we encourage producers to team up as groups and support calls for the new supermarket ombudsman to have teeth. But expanding other, more direct routes to market is crucial to the resilience of organic systems – this is where we see some of the most startling innovations, the most thorough-going commitment to organic values and the greatest ability to weather the recession. The Soil Association is doing a lot of work with our organic farmers, growers, processors and certified businesses to develop these other routes to market. This includes developing and supporting Community Supported Agriculture initiatives, where farms have a more direct link with their customers.

WANT MORE INFO?
www.soilassociation.org

ETHICAL FRUIT:
WHAT ARE THE ALTERNATIVES?

With all the problems linked to fruit growing and supply – exploitation and labour abuses, pesticides, concerns over food miles – you could easily decide to stop eating fruit and give it all a wide berth. But one bold company based in Worcestershire is convinced there is an alternative approach. *The Ecologist* quizzed **Adam Wakeley** from the ETHICAL FRUIT COMPANY to find out if it really can work.

Ecologist: *What are the typical problems linked to 'standard' fruit production that consumers should be aware of?*

> ... fruit can find its way into the market from various and numerous unregulated sources – often traded several times before ending up on the shelf.

Adam Wakeley: Conventional fruit production uses a cocktail of circa 400 different types of pesticides. The industry argues that there are Minimum Residue Levels (MRL) allowed on fruit, which are deemed to be safe – however, what is not known is the damage that a cocktail of these residue levels does when in combination with each other, which is in effect what is on the fruit (it is now known that pesticides are linked to higher rates of cancer…). In addition, fruit can find its way into the market from various and numerous unregulated sources – often traded several times before ending up on the shelf. While there is much talk of 'traceability', there is no guarantee that the growers have treated their staff fairly or ethically or have grown their fruit responsibly.

Ecologist: *How does the Ethical Fruit Company do things differently?*

AW: We adopt key principles to be adhered to by our suppliers… It must be grown without the use of artificial pesticides (the only way to guarantee this is certified organic). It must be fairly traded – our suppliers will be audited against an ethical audit. It must be grown in an environmentally friendly way. We avoid air freight wherever possible, using sea and land transport for 99.9 per cent of all our fruit.

We will only work directly with our suppliers (we don't use agents or middle men) so we know where the fruit comes from – and we visit them every year. We then residue-check all product continually to make sure that it is indeed organic, wherever it comes from. This is imperative.

Ecologist: *Some detractors will say that sourcing fruit that can be grown domestically from overseas, year-round, will always come with an environmental footprint. Shouldn't consumers just accept that some fruits should only be eaten in season?*

> … to remove overseas markets from any third world country where fruit is being grown would remove vital employment from some of the poorest societies …

AW: This is not an argument I subscribe to. Eating fruit is good for us as an important part of a balanced diet. Fact. Sea-freighting fruit around the world has an extremely small carbon footprint and has minimal environmental impact, so this argument cannot be levied against the fruit industry. From a social perspective, to remove overseas markets from any third world country where fruit is being grown would remove vital employment from some of the poorest societies that would otherwise be unable to provide work opportunities for their people.

We can only produce so much fruit domestically, and only in certain very restricted windows across the year. […] Without imported fruit, UK prices would escalate to such a level that the poorer in our society would [be unable] to afford a healthy balanced diet that included fruit.

WANT MORE INFO?
www.ethicalfruitcompany.co.uk

2 Vegetables

INTRODUCTION

One of *The Ecologist*'s most detailed investigations
of recent years has been its examination of labour
conditions for those harvesting the food we eat.
The 'Who is picking our food?' series exposed the
often appalling conditions endured by farmworkers
globally and in many different food sectors.

In the UK, our reporting revealed how migrants
– many of them Eastern European – continue to be
vulnerable to worrying levels of exploitation and
abuse, particularly those employed in the vast fresh
vegetable and salad industry. This is despite the
outrage that followed the deaths of Chinese cockle
pickers in 2004 – drowned while harvesting shellfish
– and led to a crackdown by the authorities on rogue
gangmasters across the food sector.

Our original reports on the realities of salad
cultivation are included here, along with further pieces
looking at the chemical concoctions in your veg,
ethical mushroom growing and the pioneering, young
(and radical) farmers doing things quite differently.

HARD LABOUR:
The invisible workforce toiling in our salad fields

2

Since the Morecambe Bay tragedy in 2004, which saw more than 20 Chinese workers drown while harvesting cockles off the Lancashire coast, conditions for migrant workers employed in UK agriculture have had a spotlight shone on them like never before. But although improvements have been made, exploitation and suffering continues.

The 'wild west'

The deaths led to the introduction of the Gangmasters (Licensing) Act 2004 and the establishment of the Gangmasters Licensing Authority (GLA) to regulate labour providers across the food-processing, packing, agricultural, horticultural, forestry and shellfish-gathering sectors. The GLA aims to ensure workers receive a minimum wage, adequate accommodation, safe transport, contracts and decent working conditions.

The tough stance of the agency and its operations (it uncovered more than 2,800 workers being exploited, brought ten successful prosecutions and revoked the licences of over 25 gangmasters between April 2011 and March 2012), combined with an industry 'clean up', appeared to have curtailed many of the worst abuses common a decade ago.

Back then, major horticultural regions – Lincolnshire, West Sussex, Kent – were seen, according to one industry source, as 'the wild west, with criminals and gangsters running the show and everybody turning a blind eye'.

But conditions for some migrants employed in Britain's fields, greenhouses and packing plants remain poor, with shocking exploitation continuing. Additionally, there are concerns that funding cuts as part of the Government's austerity measures could reduce the GLA's operational ability. The body has seen its budget cut by £200,000, with further cuts likely, and a reduction in staffing. The GLA itself reported that it 'faces a major challenge in seeking to prevent the exploitation of vulnerable workers with the prospect of fewer resources'.

'Treated like cattle'

'There's no justice, there's discrimination… people are treated like cattle, not human beings, I never expected it could be like this,' Irena Jaysenka tells me, before breaking down in tears. Irena, a migrant worker from Lithuania, has been employed in the UK's horticulture sector. Like thousands of others – from Poland, Romania, Bulgaria, Ukraine and beyond

– she left her homeland in order to earn a living harvesting British fruit and vegetables. But Irena says her experience – and that of others – has been marred by exploitation and harsh conditions.

'In the beginning it was fine,' she says, describing her time working in the Kent packhouse boxing up tomatoes. 'Then they brought in a computerized system for weighing the tomatoes … weigh, check, pack; weigh, check, pack … we had to do three to four punnets

in a minute. If you had three splits [of tomato packaging] in a day you were out. Everything had to look perfect – if not, you had a problem.'

Irena describes how there would be 14 people in a line, working from crates of tomatoes weighing 15–20 kg (33–44 lbs), and that they were not allowed to talk. Most days she worked between eight and nine hours, with one half-hour break; her longest shift was 14 hours. 'Line number two, that was known as the line of death,' she says.

[The Gangmasters Licensing Authority (GLA)] uncovered more than 2,800 workers being exploited, brought ten successful prosecutions and revoked the licences of over 25 gangmasters between April 2011 and March 2012 …

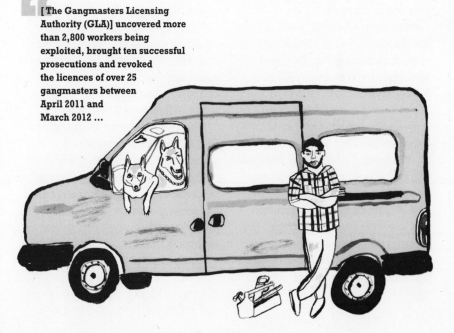

> ❝ ...safety procedures were
> 'virtually non-existent' at
> peak harvesting periods ...
> [with] pickers regularly
> complaining of suffering
> skin problems after
> harvesting plants
> without gloves or other
> protective gear.

'There was a Lithuanian supervisor and you'd be put with her to be dismissed.' Irena says that, despite being employed at the same packhouse for more than two years, packing 'thousands of punnets in a day', she was sacked after returning from a trip home. She was offered no right of reply or appeal process.

Irena found work at another Kent farm supplying fruit and vegetables to supermarkets but says treatment of migrant workers – mostly Polish, Bulgarian and Latvian – was even worse. She was paid the minimum wage – £5.93 per hour, at the time – and charged £32 per week for accommodation in a caravan, sharing with four others. She worked six days a week. She claims workers at the farm were sacked if supervisors thought they were not productive enough: 'The agency would calculate what everyone [in the team] had picked, then the least performer would be sacked,' she says.

'Systematic' exploitation

Activists say that experiences such as Irena's are far from unique, and are campaigning to force horticultural companies to employ workers on a more permanent basis, phase out casualized labour and allow unions greater access to workplaces. In a move that put the issue firmly back on the agenda, the union Unite in 2011 accused one of Britain's largest salad producers, which supplies major supermarkets, of operating 'sweatshop labour' conditions at its vast Kent greenhouse complex.

Although a subsequent GLA inquiry largely cleared the employment agencies supplying the company of any wrongdoing, Unite says problems persist, stating that some workers have no access to appropriate grievance procedures. The union says it believes exploitative practices across the horticulture sector remain 'rife'. Following the GLA enquiry, former employees – and a gangmaster – at one fruit farm in the south east alleged that migrant workers are being 'systematically' exploited, with daily dismissals for 'not performing well enough', bullying and ongoing problems with workers' pay. And a former supervisor at a salad producer in the south described living and working conditions for some workers as 'dreadful'.

'There would sometimes be eight or ten workers squeezed into a truck [caravan] designed for only four ...,' the supervisor says. 'And they are dirty, some without proper heating or beds. Sometimes [workers] would complain of having to share rooms and being kept up at night by other migrants drinking or having sex.' These workers had more than £30 deducted from their wages each week to pay for 'living in this squalor', he claimed. There have also been cases of casual workers spending the summer months 'living on the beach' to avoid incurring accommodation fees for substandard caravans.

Disregard for health & safety

The supervisor also alleged that health and safety procedures were 'virtually non-existent' at peak harvesting periods, with a number of accidents reportedly 'covered up' and pickers regularly complaining of suffering skin problems after harvesting plants without gloves or other protective gear. They blame the reactions on pesticides and other chemicals applied during cultivation.

An unpublished dossier notes that workers at the large Kent greenhouse targeted by Unite claim to have suffered rashes and skin complaints. One worker

THE INVISIBLE WORKFORCE

Figures on the precise number of migrant workers operating in the UK are hard to pinpoint, largely because of the transient nature of the sectors involved, but recent research indicated that more than 80 per cent of all peak season agricultural workers are migrants.

In 2009, the UK Border Agency estimated that at least 90,000 migrant workers had been active in the previous four years within the agriculture industry, although the total is believed to be significantly higher as workers recruited by gangmasters and employment agencies were not included. Illegal migrants – some of whom work within the sector – were also not accounted for.

cited this as a reason given by his agency for his dismissal, while others had reportedly signed a petition relating to an alleged lack of provision of drinking water in greenhouses.

A recent report by the Joseph Rowntree Foundation confirmed that many migrants working in the UK food sector continue to live in a climate of fear – subjected to inhumane conditions, racism, sexism and bullying, and forced to work long hours for less than the minimum wage.

Supermarket pressure

Pressure from major food retailers on horticultural suppliers to provide – at short notice, and around the clock – large volumes of vegetables or fruit is at least in part to blame for ongoing problems. Many suppliers rely on a highly flexible, disposable workforce in order to meet the demands of the 'just in time' ordering system adopted by large supermarkets. Growers say it's unrealistic for them to switch from using casual migrant labour because they frequently require workers for no more than six or eight months of the year and therefore need flexibility.

And industry bodies maintain that recent years have seen improvements in conditions for migrant workers. David Camp, spokesman for the Association of Labour Providers (ALP), says that following earlier scandals, all parties have worked together to tackle the problem. 'There's been a significant improvement for migrant workers receiving their rights in accordance with the law,' he said. 'We've seen a multi-stakeholder approach… the supermarkets want to do the right thing and reduce reputational risk.'

Camp acknowledges that problems still persist, however: 'What you see is jobs being advertised in native languages. This can be an entrepreneur or a gang-controlled operation. "We have work in…" they advertise, through Gumtree or migrant workers' sites. This is for a service provided – they pay to travel over, take them to the door of the labour provider, they know nothing of their backgrounds,' Camp says. He also feels that recent years had seen a switch from gangmasters being predominantly British to being foreign nationals.

The GLA, too, acknowledges that there's much work to be done: 'There's still plenty of it [exploitation] out there … you have a situation where no one wants to work in agriculture and there's large numbers of unskilled workers here,' one senior figure says.

WANT MORE INFO?
www.unitetheunion.org

'FACTORIES IN THE FIELDS'

Donna Simpson, a researcher with the Centre for Food Policy at City University, London, spent several months living and working with migrant farm workers. Her research uncovered a wide variety of experiences for migrants – some positive and some negative – and she is cautious about drawing simplistic conclusions: 'There are some farms and horticultural employers that clearly do value their seasonal workforce and make great efforts to retain them, hence the provision of good accommodation and social activities,' she says.

Despite this, Simpson said no one should be in any doubt that problems do exist, or that the work is physically tough: 'Having experienced three months of harvesting lettuce myself, I can honestly say that it was only by doing this work that I appreciated and understood the intensity of it. There are too many notions of the rural idyll and romanticism about physical work. The current work regimes in horticulture make injured robots out of people in an environment that is industrial in its scale of production. We have factories in the fields and small islands of workers living in caravans.'

NOTE: Some names have been changed.

INSIDE A SALAD 'MEGA FARM'

 In contrast to the squalid conditions faced by many migrant farm workers, employees of one large salad producer in East Anglia live in specially built hostels with a social centre, sports pitches and a bar. Is this the future of industrial horticulture?

Relentless, dirty, noisy work

The field is huge – at least the size of several football pitches combined. Along one edge is a hedge. Beyond that, another field – probably even larger – and beyond that, another. These fields, in Suffolk, UK, form part of an industrial-scale lettuce farm, one of the country's biggest. The farm supplies its vast produce – beetroot, celery, radishes, leeks and onions are also grown here – to British supermarkets, wholesalers and others in the food-processing sector.

The operation is enormous – the company behind the farm has a turnover exceeding £240 million – and in order to meet demand it employs as many as 4,500 people to cultivate and process its produce. Many of them are migrant workers, predominantly from Eastern Europe – Poland, Bulgaria, Lithuania and elsewhere.

It's mid-morning at a typical harvesting shift. The ground is very muddy. The team are harvesting 'little gem' lettuces. There are five 'rigs' at work. Rigs are essentially tractor-pulled mobile factory processing units – the type you sometimes see from the road when driving through arable country. Each rig has a crew of 21 – 10 to 12

people cutting the lettuces down below, the others working on top.

It's relentless, dirty, noisy work. The cutting team shuffles slowly along in the mud beside the moving rig; bending, cutting, bending, cutting. Upstairs, in the noisy rig bay area, the lettuces come off the conveyor belt thick and fast, straight into plastic wrapping. They'll leave the farm tonight, a worker explains, go to the depot, and be on their way to the shelves of a major supermarket chain soon after.

Industrial scale

Typically, up to 70,000 little gem lettuces are harvested here each day. On one occasion, a staggering 132,000 were picked in a single day, according to one supervisor. But despite the undeniably tough nature of the graft involved, the company concerned has a reputation for treating its workforce well, with the migrants offered regular shifts, fair pay, good living conditions and social facilities.

The main company hostel houses up to 600 workers in dormitory-style accommodation or, when at capacity, in a few nearby caravans. Each room contains six beds, a freezer and a fridge (workers cook in a separate kitchen, or eat in an onsite canteen). Couples can apply for a space in a dedicated two-person room. There's also a shop, internet café, social centre, football and basketball pitches, a tennis court and an outdoor barbecue area.

It is far from being a hotel, however – the building is more like a university hall of residence, with long corridors, artificial lighting, fire notices and communal bathrooms – but, as the company maintains, people are here to work; they're not here for a holiday. The money most earn far exceeds what they could earn in their home country.

Workers are paid on a piecework system, with payment based on results – the more work completed, the more money a worker earns – although some jobs are based on an hourly rate. The company tells me that all of its payment rates are in accordance with the national minimum wage (currently £6.19 per hour). Typically workers here earn around £250 per week, a figure that can rise for experienced – and fast – employees.

Complex process

Later, in the packhouse, a shift of workers are about to start processing and boxing up the produce coming in from the fields. Biosecurity is tight; overalls and hairnets are given out. Inside, teams of operatives are busy on production lines laid out in front of a wall containing data relating to the day's orders – how many of each product, in what format and at what price. This is where the scale of the operation becomes clear. Information is processed through to here from a team of product managers and logistics experts elsewhere in the building.

A product manager at the facility later talks me through the complex process of ensuring the company's clients – including all of the major supermarkets – receive what they want, when they want it. At 8am an order may come in for, say, 10,000 or 20,000 lettuces – by 6 or 7pm that consignment needs to have been harvested, processed, boxed up and be on its way to the depot. This is a typical time span but it can vary. The company gets paid on what it delivers. It's very rare for an order to be 'dropped' and not delivered. Night shifts are organized to cover particularly large orders or a shortfall from daytime harvesting (if not enough workers are booked in, loudspeaker messages are broadcast at the hostel asking for extra hands), alongside a 24-hour packhouse operation, if needed.

> **At 8am an order may come in for, say, 10,000 or 20,000 lettuces – by 6 or 7pm that consignment needs to have been harvested, processed, boxed up and be on its way to the depot.**

People: a key resource

Nothing is left to chance and orders are predicted; the company has a dedicated computer system for forecasting sales, taking into account myriad factors including historical order data, weather and supermarket promotions. Nothing can equip the operation for some unexpected events, however, such as a sudden sunny spell causing people to dust off their barbeques. When this happens, orders for lettuce can go through the roof.

All this explains in part why the horticulture sector – in common with most other types of agriculture – is increasingly dominated by fewer, and larger, more integrated operators. The intense, last-minute nature of modern supply chains means smaller, less well equipped outfits simply cannot cope with the demands of large retailers. The operation is in many ways the salad equivalent of the controversial 'mega farms' increasingly being touted to supply the UK's appetite for cheap pork and milk.

The product manager acknowledges that there aren't many small players any more. Despite this, he believes there are still only two key resources needed: the right soil type, and the people who make up the business. Without people, the business simply couldn't function, he says. There's no replacement for the human eye and judgement. He says that if the company didn't look after its workers, its labour source would dry up: from an ethical point of view, it's the right thing to do, he argues. The cheap gang labour of the past is simply no longer going to be good enough.

CHEMICAL WARFARE:
WHAT'S REALLY IN OUR VEG?

Most of our vegetables arrive on the supermarket shelf after being sprayed with a cocktail of chemicals during cultivation. There is increasing concern that this could pose a risk to human health, but what is the alternative and how can shoppers avoid the most problematic items? To answer some of these key questions and put the situation in perspective, *The Ecologist* spoke to **Nick Mole** from **PESTICIDE ACTION NETWORK UK (PAN UK)**, the leading body working to reduce pesticide use both in the UK and beyond.

Ecologist: *Consumers hear relatively little about the pesticides that may be used to grow their veg. What's the extent of the problem and how worried should they really be?*

For the average consumer who does not buy mainly organic, it is safe to say that the food they eat will have been grown with pesticides and may well still contain residues.

Nick Mole: In the UK, only around 5 per cent of land is under organic production, which means in effect grown without pesticides, so 95 per cent is grown using pesticides. The vast majority of the food we import is also grown using pesticides. For the average consumer who does not buy mainly organic, it is safe to say that the food they eat will have been grown with pesticides and may well still contain residues. [...] As these are invisible and odourless, it is impossible to determine which produce has residues and which doesn't! And contrary to received wisdom, washing and peeling is unlikely to remove residues as they are often contained within the whole fruit or vegetable.

Ecologist: *Most of the technical-sounding names of chemicals used in vegetable cultivation won't mean much to people. What are some of the key 'nasties' shoppers should be wary of?*

NM: That is a difficult question to give a specific answer to. Different chemicals have different potential effects and can of course affect people in different ways. […] However, it is clear that certain food items are more likely to contain one or more pesticide residues and some are more prone to this than others. If you are worried about consuming residues, PAN UK would recommend you buy organic versions of the worst offenders, such as oranges, grapes, apples, tomatoes, carrots and lettuce.

Ecologist: *Just how much of a health risk does pesticide usage in conventional vegetable growing really pose?*

NM: It is difficult to say and hard not to sound alarmist. […] That said, there is a growing body of evidence to suggest that prolonged exposure [to pesticides and residues] can have harmful effects on health, particularly for vulnerable groups such as babies, children, pregnant women and the elderly. As an example, a 2012 study by the US environmental news service EcoWatch showed that women exposed to certain agricultural pesticides gave birth to children with lower birth weights.

> ... a 2012 study by the US environmental news service EcoWatch showed that women exposed to certain agricultural pesticides gave birth to children with lower birth weights.

Ecologist: *Shoppers can buy organic if they can afford it, but shouldn't the food producers, retailers – and indeed the authorities – be doing more to reduce pesticide use?*

NM: PAN UK believes much more should and could be done […]. Some retailers are taking the issue seriously and working to reduce the use of some pesticides and residues in the products they sell. However, […] there needs to be a radical move away from the current thinking of pesticides first to a 'pesticides last and only if all other non-chemical techniques have failed' approach. This needs to be adopted by growers and farmers with support from government and retailers to help them adopt new chemical-free approaches to crop production.

WANT MORE INFO?
www.pan-uk.org

MAGIC MUSHROOMS

In an attempt to limit the environmental impacts of mushroom farming, one organic Welsh grower is focusing on local sourcing, growing, delivery – and consumption. Shunning the use of toxic chemicals and tools imported from the other side of the world, **Gary Whiteley** from **MAESYFFIN MUSHROOMS** tells *The Ecologist* how he does it.

Ecologist: *Most consumers probably have little idea of how mushrooms are grown. Could you tell us what the basic cultivation processes are?*

Gary Whiteley: Most cultivated mushrooms need a heat-treated substrate to grow on. What this substrate is depends upon the kind of mushroom being grown. Some grow on composted horse manure, while others require wood, cardboard, straw, used coffee grounds or other waste materials. A spawn culture is made (usually on either grain or sawdust) and the substrate is inoculated with the spawn and left to incubate, so that the mushroom mycelium grows into, and feeds from, the host. Depending on the necessary conditions of humidity, temperature and light (yes, most mushrooms require light to grow!), eventually fruiting bodies (mushrooms) will be produced for harvest.

Ecologist: *What problems, from a sustainability point of view, can be associated with 'conventionally' grown mushrooms?*

GW: Both 'conventional' and other mushroom cultivation operations require some heat, so when the seasons are cold this requires energy – in my case, electricity from a green energy supplier. Obviously we all need to bring materials to our sites, but since these are mostly waste products, it could be argued that all mushroom producers are to a larger extent sustainable, though transport costs may be a major factor for larger, centralized producers. Mushrooms could be grown on a small local scale in towns and cities using available waste streams (e.g. coffee grounds and cardboard) to provide fresh nutritious foods all year round.

Ecologist: *Maesyffin Mushrooms markets itself as being genuinely locally sourced and grown – what makes you different from many ordinary growers?*

GW: I'm just trying to do things properly, not looking to be different. Local sourcing, growing, delivery and consumption mean lower food miles and a smaller carbon footprint for all of us – producer, retailer and consumer. [The provenance of my product is transparent], which isn't usually the case where mushrooms are labelled 'UK grown' but the fruiting substrates are made abroad and imported into the UK to be grown and harvested. Here I make use of locally grown organic grains, brash from a local organic farm, sawdust from a local joinery and organic bran from Felin Ganol, a restored local watermill. Additionally, my vehicle is largely powered by biodiesel, home-made from locally collected used cooking oil.

Ecologist: *Just how important is organic cultivation in terms of protecting the environment?*

GW: It means no chemicals, no preservatives, no poisons. So wildlife is better protected and there are no toxic residues to affect human health. Also, waste products such as animal slurry or, in my case, used fruiting blocks – which in the first place are made largely from local waste wood materials (chipped tree brash and waste sawdust) – can be composted and reused to supplement organic materials on the land.

> Local sourcing, growing, delivery and consumption mean lower food miles and a smaller carbon footprint for all of us – producer, retailer and consumer.

Ecologist: *Finally – and importantly! – does an organic, ethically produced, mushroom really taste any better?*

GW: As I don't eat anyone's mushrooms but my own, I can't comment directly. But the feedback I get from my customers […] means there must be something about my mushrooms that keeps them coming back. Organic and ethical principles, quality, freshness, love and attention to detail must all help to provide a great taste experience.

WANT MORE INFO?
www.maesymush.co.uk

COULD HORSEPOWER BE THE FUTURE OF FARMING?

Deep in Devon, a radical experiment in community-supported agriculture is showing how it's possible to produce food locally and sustainably while breaking our reliance on fossil fuel guzzling farming methods. But does it stack up?

Rural England

The countryside around the village of Chagford, on the edge of Dartmoor in Devon, is the stuff of picture postcards. Rolling hills, thick forests, deep valleys, gushing streams and lots of farms. Village noticeboards carry posters advertising the local hunt's forthcoming events. Passing 4x4 vehicles are ablaze with field sports stickers. This is traditional, rural England, where country pastimes remain popular and meddling by outsiders is frowned upon.

But the noticeboards here are also dotted with posters hinting at a very different community. One announces a course in 'Goddesses' – workshops where participants apparently use 'myth, journeying, movement and creativity'. Another has details on a local allotment scheme and how to get involved. In the village centre there's a busy wholefood café and health food shop that sells lots of vegetarian and vegan food. There are adverts on the wall for organic smallholdings for sale in Spain. Three people queueing up for food are talking about the spiritual retreat – and associated detox – that they've just been enjoying locally.

> **Shareholders receive a full box of produce between June and December – the bountiful months – and a smaller clutch of items in the leaner times between January and May, all grown locally on land leased by Chagfood.**

Community-supported food

Ed Hamer is a radical young farmer, land rights activist and driving force behind a pioneering Community Supported Agriculture (CSA) scheme – Chagfood, based at Easton Cross just outside Chagford itself – that's attracting attention because of its rejection of conventional, oil-based farming methods in favour of traditional horsepower. Everyone in here seems to know him – the planned Chagfood open day has just been postponed because of bad weather; people are asking when it'll be rearranged for – and those that don't will almost certainly have heard of him.

Ed explains how Chagfood supplies seasonal fruit and vegetables to a growing number of local households on a weekly basis, with the recipients paying an annual subscription fee of up to £600 to secure their share of produce for the year ahead. This unique upfront payment is partly what makes the venture stand out from more typical box schemes, where consumers generally pick and choose when and what to buy.

The financial commitment helps Ed, and co-founder and business partner Chinnie Kingsbury, to plan and bankroll the year's cultivation. It also means – as is central to the ethos behind community-supported agriculture projects – that the risks and rewards of production are more equally shared between consumer and producer.

'In 2010, we supplied 25 weekly boxes from 1 acre of land; in 2011 it was 50 [boxes] from 2 acres, last year it was 75 boxes from 3 acres,' he says. 'This year we are planning to increase this further… but not [by] too much.' Shareholders receive a full box of produce between June and December – the bountiful months – and a smaller clutch of items in the leaner times between January and May, all grown locally on land leased by Chagfood.

THE SUBSIDY SCANDAL

The European Union's controversial Common Agricultural Policy (CAP), originally set up to ensure a steady supply of food for European consumers and help farmers receive a fair income, sees more than 50 billion euros paid out annually in subsidies to farmers across Europe. Critics point out that this currently takes up more than 40 per cent of the EU's annual budget and amounts to the equivalent of each EU citizen paying out 100 euros per year. The CAP is also criticized as a large amount of its payments go to the biggest farms, while many smaller producers struggle on low incomes.

www.farmsubsidy.org

❝ ... Chagfood is financially self-supporting and covers two modest wages and the essential operating costs, which are kept low in part by the deployment of horsepower.

Chagfood wouldn't be possible, however, without the physical assistance of the shareholders and other supporters. 'Each week we have between 10 and 15 people helping out,' says Ed. 'It's about the community aspect and the cultural side of farming, a side that's been lost... We have harvest [festival] and a spring festival; and the kids are always involved.'

Voluntary support

The venture began in 2009 after a public meeting organized by a think-tank, the New Economics Foundation (NEF), found that a cross-section of the local community wanted to try to 'shorten the distance' between food producers and consumers. A core group – Ed and Chinnie, supported by an enthusiastic body of friends and volunteers – rented a small plot from a sympathetic farmer and prepared the ground for sowing. The project secured financial backing from a number of sources, including the Big Lottery Fund's local food programme, enabling the purchase of essential tools and helping to underwrite costs.

Horse-drawn power

With the scheme now in its fourth year, Ed confirms that Chagfood is financially self-supporting and covers two modest wages and the essential operating costs, which are kept low in part by the deployment of horsepower. Chagfood uses Samson, a Dartmoor x Welsh Cob, to carry out most of the cultivation of its fields and to transport its produce.

Samson works the fields – the original site has been joined by another field leased from a local organic farm – attached to a tillage device known as the Pioneer Homesteader. Ed imported the old-fashioned yet sturdy-looking device from an Amish community in the US: 'It's similar to a Massey Ferguson tractor… it straddles the bed [and can have] several different tools attached. It's the principle of mechanization applied to horses.'

Industrial agribusiness

Ed's enthusiasm for horsepower runs deeper than simple financial calculations – as well as being a farmer, he's co-editor of the radical *The Land* magazine and a founder of the campaign group Reclaim the Fields, which seeks to empower those seeking greater access to land. He argues that conventional farming and agribusiness in the UK is fundamentally flawed because of its reliance on EU financial subsidies, and says that two of the biggest hurdles facing those wanting to get into farming are access to both land and appropriate skills.

The farmer believes that – stripping it all down – what Chagfood is actually doing is just growing food and selling it at a realistic price: 'It's the real cost of food, our costs are the same since we started, compared with the supermarket [prices, which fluctuate],' he says. 'We're able to tailor production to local demand. Local food schemes [like this] are more resilient, we're not plugged into the food infrastructure. We are connecting people to local food.'

WANT MORE INFO?
www.chagfood.org.uk

GROW!
THE YOUNG FARMERS STANDING UP TO 'BIG AG'

The US is the spiritual and financial home of big agriculture, and a base for some of the world's most powerful food companies. But it's also the setting for a quiet revolution that is seeing a new and more radical breed of farmer take up the (organic, sustainable) plough in a show of defiance to conventional (pesticide, oil-driven) agribusiness. To better understand this trend, *The Ecologist* spoke with **Christine Anthony** and **Owen Masterson**, the filmmakers behind **GROW!**, a landmark documentary featuring 20 young maverick farmers from across Georgia who are employing a new and sustainable approach to growing food.

Ecologist: *How many young farmers are rejecting mainstream agriculture and going it alone down the alternative, organic route?*

Christine Anthony & Owen Masterson: The last official figures are from 2007 and since then there has been a huge increase in new and beginning farmers which would include young farmers, refugees and one of the fastest growing demographics: women farmers. […] This is a movement taking place all over the US and Canada. […] No matter which state we showed [the film] in, the young farmers in the audience could relate to and identify with everything said by the farmers in GROW! An interesting trend […] is

> **An interesting trend is young [farmers] persuading their parents to switch their [conventional] operations over to organic and sustainable agriculture.**

> **Consumers are the ones who must really offer support and help to change the system by buying directly from these growers at farmers' markets, through Community Supported Agriculture … and by supporting local businesses …**

young people persuading their parents […] to switch their [conventional] operations over to organic and sustainable agriculture.

Ecologist: *Do you think this new group of young farmers has the power to (eventually) challenge the grip of big agriculture and corporate farming?*

CA & OM: Nobody is naive enough to think that the small, sustainable type of agriculture will replace big ag but that is not the intention […]. What is interesting and where this kind of agriculture is really gaining ground is on a local level. It's not going to happen in one big plough over, but as more and more communities embrace and support this movement, eventually all of these communities have the potential to overlap and really have a strong negative impact on big ag. This movement is also already beginning to have an impact on Big Food (major food corporations) who are now

co-opting some of the buzz words like 'local', 'naturally raised' and 'farmer owned', stretching the truth to signify something that is not exactly local, natural or farmer owned.

Ecologist: *What support – from government, industry, civil society – would best secure the future of independent young farmers in the US?*

CA & OM: Unfortunately, because the economy is such a wreck, a lot of the funding for grants from the [US government] that [has] been in place to help small and beginning farmers has been shrinking. Consumers are the ones who must really offer support and help to change the system by buying directly from these growers at farmers' markets. Or, they can buy through Community Supported Agriculture (where the consumer gives the farmer money at the beginning of the season for the produce that will be grown and distributed to the consumer when the crops are harvested) and by supporting local businesses such as restaurants and grocery stores that purchase produce from their local farmers. Another way that people can help is by engaging their politicians on a local, state and national level and encouraging them to put policies and funding into place to help small, sustainable farmers.

WANT MORE INFO?
www.growmovie.net

3 Meat & Fish

INTRODUCTION

When it comes to meat, it's been the standard line for environmentalists: eat less of it, and when you do make sure it's only the highest quality, the highest welfare, strictly organic and locally produced.

The Ecologist itself has advocated such an approach at different times in its lengthy history, either because of an editor's individual preference, or for wider marketing and advertising purposes. But such a stance has always proved controversial and polarizing, particularly as the magazine has probably devoted more time and resources to investigating meat – and all the related moral, environmental and social issues – than just about anything else. And the findings haven't been pretty – physically speaking, in the case of the various welfare scandals we've reported on.

But, as the selection of pieces here highlight, there are many other reasons to rethink meat consumption, including its often overlooked impact on people (particularly those living near to factory farms) and the environment – entire ecosystems are under threat, in fact.

INSIDE AN INDUSTRIAL PIG FACTORY

3

Squalid conditions and rampant use of controversial drugs are typical of the intensive concentrated animal feeding operations (CAFOs) that supply much of the pork consumed today. But it's not only animals that suffer – people do too, especially those living near to factory farms.

Squalor & filth

Beyond a dense strip of forest off a narrow, single-track road in remote countryside is what looks to be a man-made fishing lake. But it soon becomes clear that this is no ordinary lake. It is an open cesspit, a giant lagoon full to bursting with waste from the nearby industrial-scale pig farm.

Floating beneath the surface are the bodies of an unidentifiable number – dozens, perhaps hundreds – of dead pigs and piglets in various states of decomposition. Until their carcasses are prised out of the waste, they are almost unrecognizable aside from the odd snout and curly tail visible in the filth. Everywhere is the detritus of industrial factory farming – plastic syringe casings, intravenous needles and white clinical gloves – floating in the rancid cesspit and discarded on adjacent farmland.

Welcome to an industrial pig-rearing factory – or, as they are known in the US, a concentrated animal feeding operation (CAFO). This CAFO, in Poland, belongs to a major pork producer that supplies

> **Floating beneath the surface are the bodies of an unidentifiable number – dozens, perhaps hundreds – of dead pigs and piglets in various states of decomposition.**

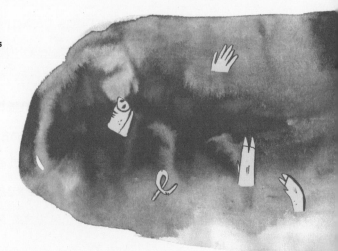

meat to the catering sector and to supermarkets across Europe and the US – and well beyond. It is typical of intensive pig farms the world over. The company running the farm claims to operate with stringent regard for animal welfare, the environment and for the communities in which they work. But, like so much of what the agribusiness industry says, the reality doesn't match the rhetoric.

Emaciated, sick & weak

At another farm, there is an intensive piglet 'nursery', where younger animals are brought from breeding establishments elsewhere to grow before being dispatched to the slaughterhouse. Beyond the barbed wire and military-style security lies a series of giant sheds, each containing hundreds of pigs. The animals appear to have no access to outdoor exercise or daylight. In one building, under dazzling artificial light, there is evidence of lame and injured animals. Some

appear emaciated, others are clearly sick and some are very frail. Live pigs surround the carcasses of abandoned dead ones.

In common with CAFOs the world over that house pigs or other farm animals, the company involved here routinely administers an extensive cocktail of medicines, including controversial antibiotics. Although

THE ANTIBIOTICS TIME BOMB

The effect on human health of antibiotics used in intensive farming has recently become an issue of public debate.

Bacteria living in animals can quickly become resistant to antibiotics. The antibiotics used in human medicine are often similar – if not identical – to those used in farming, and bacteria are able to transmit their resistant qualities to humans very easily. The bacteria then become resistant to the antibiotics used to treat human illnesses.

Drugs cleared for dispensing in this Polish CAFO included Tylbian 20%, understood to be a form of tylosin, controversial and banned throughout the EU as a growth promoter due to concerns about cross-resistance; lincomycin, never licensed in at least one country – the UK – as a growth promoter because it is cross-resistant with another drug, clindamycin, used in human medicine; and Stresnil, a powerful sedative.

officially administered in an attempt to limit the spread of illness and disease, some of the antibiotics have a growth-promoting side effect.

Pollution & waste

The arrival of pig CAFOs in Poland has also led to conflict between the multinational firms behind them and local communities. In the village housing the piglet 'nursery', locals told us the farm, which contains as many as 13,000 animals, now dominates the whole area.

One of the first serious complaints from community members following the farm's establishment was the regular movement through the village of heavy trucks loaded with dead animals from the premises. It was later reported that overcrowding inside the farm led to the deaths of hundreds of pigs – their carcasses dumped outside until a protest led to their removal.

According to residents, the pig farm's creation was accompanied by the arrival of an overpowering, unrelenting stench from piles of waste created by the animals. Giant dumps of pig manure appeared in wheat fields adjacent to the installation, with waste reportedly draining onto the shores of a nearby lake used for swimming by the local community. Eye infections in those who swam in the lake were reported.

One resident, a zoological technician who has lived here for over 30 years, told us that the smell from the waste dumps became so bad that school-

" ... the smell from the waste dumps became so bad that schoolchildren could no longer open classroom windows for fear of vomiting ...

children could no longer open classroom windows for fear of vomiting, and that people living close by complained of nausea and blackouts. When we visited the stench was still apparent, although the farm appeared to be housing at least some of the waste inside the perimeter of the installation.

The residents tell us that the farm's operators offered money to purchase new windows for the school in an attempt to alleviate the problems, but that the community refused, fearing that the company might use acceptance of the goodwill gesture to suggest that everything was OK.

Water contamination

Another resident living downwind from a nearby CAFO operated by the same company says that people have struggled with water contamination and appalling smells since the farm was established. This farm contains up to 10,000 breeding sows. According to the resident, an official health inspection previously discovered that nitrogen levels in drinking water were three times higher than the permitted levels, with a local lake closed because of contamination with *E.coli* bacteria.

In a secret visit to the pig farm, we were shown giant open-air waste lagoons concealed near wheat fields behind the installation, and tractors spreading waste onto nearby farmland. Local people blame this for contamination and pollution incidents.

Residents acknowledge that some steps have been taken to minimize the farm's impact – and that pressure led to the postponement of construction of a second farm in the region – but maintain that there is continued anger that public money was used to install a separate water system in the region following the problems. They also say local people continue to question why all this is necessary for 'cheap meat' – much of it destined for foreign shores and not eaten locally.

WANT MORE INFO?
www.pigbusiness.co.uk

THE GAME MEAT HOAX

3

Touted as wild, free range and ethically produced, game meat has become increasingly popular in recent years. But a brutal cycle of factory farming and persecution of wildlife lies behind the supply of pheasants, partridges and other game birds.

Big business battery farming

Deep in the Welsh countryside, well away from the road and prying eyes, lies a farm. Vast, factory-style buildings, feed towers and wire enclosures spread across the valley. Tractors are moving around in the distance; closer by, a group of workers are loading a van.

But despite appearances, this is no ordinary farm. It is the UK's largest game-bird rearing facility, supplying pheasants and partridges to shooting estates across the country. Situated away from the main buildings are the breeding units – row upon row of tiny metal cages, in which the birds, unable to fly or touch the ground, appear to endure a shockingly cruel and miserable existence.

The company behind this Welsh farm claims to churn out more than 300,000 game bird chicks per week and up to a million poults – young birds – per year across its business. They are supplied

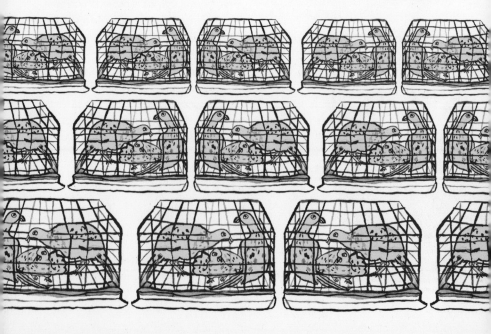

to gamekeepers who then rear the birds on country estates until they are ready for releasing ahead of the annual shooting season each autumn.

From September (for partridge) and October (for pheasant) to the end of January, groups of game shooting enthusiasts – or 'guns', as they are known in the industry – pay to blast these birds from the sky for sport. Britain's shooting industry is a multimillion pound business that sees between 35 and 40 million game birds reared annually for shooting at around 2,000 different estates.

The shoots themselves vary enormously – ranging from 'private' days at magnificent country houses to highly expensive 'corporate' packages on dedicated shooting grounds, to small 'rough' shoots on the edge of major towns or cities. The costs vary, but estates can charge up to £10,000 for a day's shooting for a group of eight 'guns'.

'Wild, free range & locally produced'

At the end of a day's shooting, some birds – particularly after large, 'corporate' shoots – are dumped in specially designed pits or simply discarded in the countryside. (This controversial practice was long denied by the shooting fraternity until undercover investigations at a number of shooting estates proved it was happening.) But many shot birds are now sold into the food chain. Some are exported to feed demand in European countries, others serve a growing UK market.

This game meat is increasingly touted as wild, natural, free range and locally produced; an ethical and healthy meat that offers a viable alternative to mass-produced, factory-reared produce. In recent years, the shooting lobby has embarked on a slick marketing exercise – garnering

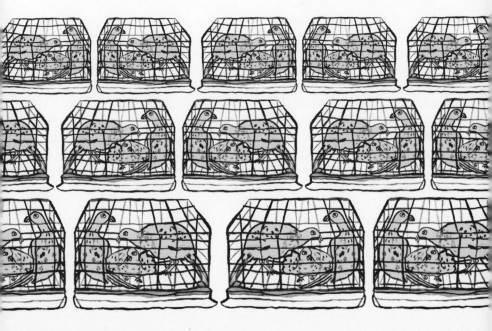

support from a range of celebrity chefs and others – to persuade the public of the merits of game.

This has resulted in something of a boom in popularity, with game popping up at farmers' markets, butchers, delicatessens and – increasingly – supermarkets. The sector is among the fastest growing across the meat industry.

But consumers are being misled. Game meat is linked to a brutal cycle of factory farming, poor husbandry and other animal welfare abuses at breeding farms across the UK and overseas. Added to this, the intensive breeding results in some game birds being administered drugs, including antibiotics, and specially designed feed that often contains genetically modified (GM) ingredients – inputs few would associate with 'wild, natural' meat.

Cannibalism & cruelty

The Welsh farm is just one of about half a dozen similar establishments in the UK believed to be utilizing battery-style systems to maximize productivity.

Intensive systems such as this cause considerable stress to captive birds, say campaigners, often resulting in abnormal behaviours including cannibalism. Undercover filming has revealed appalling injuries suffered by some game birds held in intensive facilities, as well as deformities, sickness and apparent negligence by some staff, with dead or injured birds left lying around unattended to.

In addition to these 'superfarms', dozens of smaller facilities also rear birds for supply to the shooting industry, with conditions often little better than their bigger counterparts. Indeed some of the worst husbandry has been uncovered at small farms where staffing, equipment and expertise is likely to be lacking and where scrutiny by third parties is less likely.

A growing number of game birds shot on UK estates and subsequently put into the food chain are thought to originate from intensive farms elsewhere in Europe. It has been estimated that as many as 40 per cent of pheasants and

90 per cent of partridges released in the UK are imported as chicks or eggs, mostly from France. Others originate in Spain, Denmark and even the US.

In some cases, French factory farms utilizing battery-style cages have been found to supply UK game dealers. These in turn supply birds to shooting estates but also retrieve the carcasses from those shoots for processing and onward sale as game meat, both direct to the public via farmers' markets and butchers, and to restaurants. Some supermarket chains, which often market their game products as free range, have also been linked to game meat suppliers who source birds from shooting estates known to buy from game farms using battery-style breeding techniques.

Given the increasing scrutiny our food chains now face, critics say it is surprising – and worrying – that the game meat sector has been allowed to misrepresent itself to consumers for so long. In any other sector there would have been an outcry – followed by a firm clampdown on those peddling the lies.

THE QUAIL TRAIL

Quail meat and eggs have become increasingly popular treats among foodie circles. The meat from these tiny birds is often roasted and found on the menus of upmarket restaurants, while the eggs are sometimes served poached, boiled or fried as an alternative to conventional eggs, or offered as an unusual addition to canapés. Quail is often sold alongside other game products – including pheasant, partridge and guinea fowl – and is similarly marketed as wild, natural and wholly ethical.

However, many quail are in fact reared highly intensively, either in broiler-chicken type conditions (for meat) – with birds crammed into windowless sheds without access to the outdoors – or in tiny, filthy, battery-style wire cages (for eggs) that prevent birds from exhibiting their natural behaviour.

Investigations at UK and Spanish quail farms in recent years have uncovered conditions described as 'appalling' and 'cruel', with dead and injured birds found lying among the living and many having virtually no feathers left after being pecked by other birds. In the UK, quail eggs from a major supplier were pulled from the shelves of several top food retailers after footage of such conditions was released.

SOYA WARS

3

Much of the cheap meat and dairy produce sold in supermarkets is arriving as a result of human rights abuses and environmental damage in South America. The link? Factory-farmed animals are routinely fed a diet containing vast quantities of soya, and the crop's cultivation is increasingly leading to conflict between local communities and agribusiness.

Feeding factory farms

Soya is increasingly prized for use in farmed animal feed as it provides a cheap source of protein for poultry, pigs and other intensively reared animals that require fast growth in order to produce large meat, egg and milk yields. Globally, as much as 90 per cent of soymeal produced is now used for animal feed.

But soya plantations in Paraguay are responsible for a catalogue of social and ecological problems, including the forced eviction of rural communities, landlessness, poverty, excessive use of pesticides, deforestation and rising food insecurity.

Attracted by cheap land prices, poor environmental regulations and monitoring, widespread corruption and low taxation on agricultural export commodities, agribusinesses have long viewed Paraguay as an ideal country in which to do business. In recent decades, increasing chunks of rural land have been bought up and turned over to export-orientated soya cultivation.

Paraguay is one of the largest producers of soya, with millions of hectares of land given over to cultivating the crop. Vast quantities are exported to neighbouring Argentina, from where much of the crop is shipped to China to supply the country's growing demand for animal feed. The EU is the second largest importer of Paraguayan soya.

Deforestation & displacement

The arrival of export-orientated soya production has led to significant swathes of forest being destroyed to make way for crops, according to critics, threatening biodiversity and depleting resources vital for many rural communities. And it is estimated that, since the beginning of the soya boom in Paraguay in 1990, as many as 100,000 small-scale farmers have been forced to migrate to cities – with about 9,000 rural families evicted annually because of soya production.

Industrial-scale soya production, particularly for genetically modified (GM) crops – some 90 per cent of Paraguay's soya is thought to be GM – is dependent on the application of pesticides and other agrochemicals.

Crop spraying has polluted important water sources in many rural regions, say campaigners, poisoning both domestic and wild animals, threatening plant life, and resulting in a number of health problems in people. Pressure groups suggest that as much as 23 million litres of pesticides and herbicides are sprayed in Paraguay each year, including several classified by the World Health Organization (WHO) as 'extremely hazardous'.

Violence & killings

Paraguay has a long history of land conflict, and the arrival of large scale soya farming has been met with resistance from many rural communities. Peasant and indigenous organizations have repeatedly protested against the encroachment of their land, organizing protests, blockades, land occupations and actions to prevent pesticide spraying.

But the response from soya farmers – reportedly under the protection of police and soldiers acting on the orders of the authorities – has been brutal, according to peasant leaders, with violent evictions, shootings and beatings, disappearances and arbitrary detentions. In one of the worst recorded incidents, during the forced eviction of the peasant community at Tekojoja, in Caaguazú region, soya farmers forcibly removed some 270 people from the village, including children, arrested 130, set fire to crops and bulldozed houses, before shooting dead two inhabitants.

WANT MORE INFO?
www.foe.co.uk

THE HIDDEN COST OF SALMON

3

The production of a key ingredient in feed given to farmed salmon is devastating marine life, human health and whole ecosystems along Peru's Pacific coast.

A dirty enterprise

It is a life of poverty and filth. Standing above the tangle of rusting metal pipes and concrete-rimmed pools that lead into the ocean, Segundo Vorges and Luis Diaz explain how they scratch a living here in Chimbote harbour, Peru. They are part of a twilight community of 'pipe people' who survive by reclaiming waste discharged from nearby fishmeal production plants.

When operational, the pipes carry effluent – an unsavoury mixture of fish bodies, scales and fat – into the pools and the sea. Vorges and Diaz skim off the useful waste, particularly the fat, before shovelling it into containers. Some is turned into pellets used for cooking and sold at nearby markets. Whole families, including children, are involved in this dirty enterprise, earning £2 per day.

Despite some nasty-looking substances festering in the pools,

the 'pipe people' maintain they are unconcerned about potential risks – unlike the environmentalists, who claim such effluent contaminates the sea. 'Whatever the job is, it's work,' says Vorges. 'We need to bring money to the table.'

This shocking scene is a million miles from the succulent pink salmon fish-steaks on sale across the western world. But the two are inextricably linked: much of the fishmeal and oil produced in Peru from anchovy fish stocks is the principal ingredient of feed used in salmon farming.

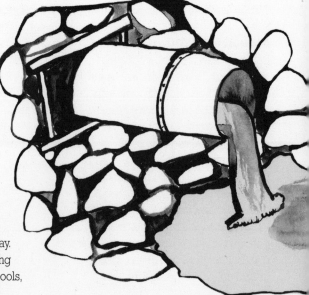

Aquaculture has for many years been targeted by pressure groups who are concerned at its apparent unsustainability and ecological footprint. But there are also serious environmental and social costs – including pollution and health problems, overfishing and impacts on ecosystems and wildlife – arising from the production of fishmeal and fish oil in Peru.

Feeding salmon farms

Fishmeal is a protein-rich flour produced by cooking, drying and milling raw fish and trimmings. Fish oil is a by-product of fishmeal processing. Both are largely derived from oily fish including anchovies, herrings and sardines. High nutritional values – both contain omega-3 fatty acids, beneficial both to humans and animals – have led to massive demand from the aquaculture industry.

Globally, the sector is worth well over $2 billion, with some 400 plants producing approximately six million tonnes of fishmeal and one million

tonnes of fish oil annually. Principal fisheries supplying producers of meal and oil are situated in European waters and in the Pacific bordering Peru and Chile. Peru is the world's leading exporter, supplying salmon farming regions in Chile, Canada, Scotland and Norway, among others.

After processing, meal and oil is usually exported for mixing with binders, such as soya, for output as feed pellets. Salmon are carnivorous and require large amounts of feed: environmentalists estimate 4 kg (9 lbs) of wild-caught fish are required to produce 1 kg (2 lbs) of farmed fish, fuelling claims that aquaculture is not sustainable.

Peru's Pacific waters contain a vital fishery and one of the world's most biologically productive coastal 'upwelling' ecosystems. Coastal 'upwelling' occurs when deep oceanic currents collide with sharp coastal shelves and force nutrient-rich cool water to the surface. The nutrients support the proliferation of phytoplankton, which in turn provide sustenance for enormous schools of anchovy and other marine animals.

Pollution & illness

In Chimbote, one of the world's most important fishmeal hubs, some 40 fishmeal plants process anchovies caught by the city's fishing fleets. At one community we visited there, more than a dozen women and children gathered to vent their anger, claiming the plants that loom over their houses are responsible for respiratory and skin problems, particularly in children.

'We know the factories are responsible […], because when it operates the illnesses get worse,' says one young woman. 'When the smoke comes it gets so bad we need a mask.' Another says that when the plants are operating the pollution is so thick you cannot physically remain on the street.

Dr Ramon de la Cruz, dean of Chimbote's Colegio Medico del Consejo Regional XIX, told us: 'As the fishing season increases, the production of fishmeal begins, and this immediately and fundamentally accentuates in the infantile population the occurrences of asthma.'

Although fishmeal production is now restricted to fixed periods, corresponding with reduced fishing seasons, community members say the industry continues to make their lives a misery. Local people also claim that buffer zones designed to separate processing plants from dwellings are being disregarded.

'These people deserve more than to be subjected to this,' says Maria Elena Foronda Farro of NGO Natura, which campaigns to resolve the problems associated with fishmeal production. 'It's even worse because this fishmeal is being processed for salmon farmed and consumed abroad.'

During a tour of a row of dilapidated classrooms in a Chimbote school afflicted by the industry, teacher Yolanda Lara tells us: 'We had to build walls to keep [smoke] out. We used to hold classes here, but the smoke, noise and pollution were so bad we can no longer use them.' Other schools have suffered too, with as many as 5,000 pupils affected by the pollution.

Dead zones

Romolo Loayza Aguila, a biologist from the city's Universidad Nacional del Santa, says that research shows how untreated effluents from fishmeal plants are contributing to serious contamination of the Bay of Ferrol off Chimbote's coast. He claims the impacts of the waste on the bay's biodiversity 'have been dramatic', as the area was 'rich in species and also in biomass'.

According to ecological group Mundo Azul, the Bay

of Ferrol is among the most polluted marine areas of the country: 'The [fishmeal] plants are discharging protein, fat and oil into the bay's water, as well as contaminated marine water used during the process of pumping the fish from the ship's hull to the processing plant.' The group claims that this, combined with contaminants deposited by air pollution, raw sewage and discharge from the steel industry, has led to the accumulation of a toxic layer of undecomposed, organic material on the sea bed, creating a marine 'dead zone'.

Dead zones are areas where algae blooms, and, although they can occur naturally, are often triggered by nutrients from fertilizer run-off, sewage, animal and industrial wastes, and atmospheric deposition from the burning of fossil fuels, removing oxygen from the water. Low levels of oxygen make it difficult for fish and other marine creatures, as well as important habitats such as sea-grass beds, to survive. The UN recently warned that such areas can threaten fish stocks.

Declining catches

Other parts of Peru's coastline have also been contaminated by waste from the fishmeal industry – fishermen believe such pollution has led to a reduction in artisanal fish catches, but they also blame the activities of industrial anchovy fleets.

Fishing chiefs and campaigners say the volume of anchovy taken for fishmeal negatively impacts the ocean's wider food chain, and thus the availability of other, previously plentiful species fished for human consumption. They also claim spawning grounds are damaged by industrial fishing. 'Fish is the basic food in Peru, but now there is not enough for local people,' says Manuel Montesa Arroyo, a spokesman for Chimbote's artisanal fishermen. 'We catch less because there are more fleets. There is [now] more deprivation as we catch less.'

Arroyo says that although laws exist to prevent industrial fishing within a 5-mile zone of the coast to protect artisanal food resources, enforcement is weak and breaches are frequent. In 2006, local media reportedly

> **As the fishing season increases, the production of fishmeal begins, and this immediately and fundamentally accentuates in the infantile population the occurrences of asthma.**

filmed as many as 50 industrial vessels fishing just metres off the beach. According to eyewitnesses, harbour authorities took no action 'because they had no fuel'.

Javier Castro, who represents the industrial fishing industry in Chimbote, admits that the sector is 'anarchic' and that frequent breaches of the law occur, with regular instances of fishing vessels manipulating satellite positioning technology to mask their positions when operating inside exclusion zones or closed seasons.

Disputed claims

Campaigners cite official research as evidence of the precarious status of anchovy stocks in the South East Pacific: the UN Food and Agriculture Organization (FAO) characterized the Peruvian

anchovy fishery as 'fully fished', meaning it has been exploited to the maximum safe biological limit. The FAO previously noted two main stocks of anchovy in the South East Pacific are 'fully exploited and overexploited'.

But the fishmeal industry maintains that anchovy stocks are carefully monitored and industrial fleets controlled through vigorous enforcement. The International Fishmeal and Fish Oil Organisation (IFFO) states that Peruvian anchovy fishing is subjected to 'comprehensive management controls to protect the stock from overfishing'. It says the Peruvian government adopts a 'precautionary approach' to regulating catches, with controls including closed seasons, net-size restrictions, vessel licensing, catch quotas and restricted fishing areas.

The IFFO also points to the satellite tracking system as further evidence of the framework in place to prevent overfishing, as well as the existence of strict codes of conduct for industrial fishing vessels. The body says Peru is an 'excellent example of a country that heeded earlier warnings on overfishing, conducted extensive research and introduced controls and third-party surveillance'.

Most recently, the fishmeal industry has said that environmental impacts are being reduced in Peru, with the IFFO stating that its members were building a waste water treatment facility and new pipeline in Chimbote to safely discharge water offshore.

❝ ...although laws exist to prevent industrial fishing within a 5-mile zone of the coast to protect artisanal food resources, enforcement is weak and breaches are frequent.

PERU'S PHANTOM FISH

Following the original *Ecologist* investigation into Peru's fishmeal industry, international watchdog groups and campaigners began to examine what was happening there. In 2012, the International Consortium of Investigative Journalists (ICIJ) claimed that at least 630,000 metric tonnes of anchoveta vanished between 2009 and 2011 – 'lost' somewhere between boat holds and the scales of fishmeal plants and other processing factories.

The 'phantom' fish were simply not counted, says the group, allowing companies to evade taxes and overfish their quotas. Fishermen, usually paid for what they catch in weight, were then effectively cheated out of their earnings. The ICIJ analysed data for more than 100,000 different anchoveta landings in Peru dating back to 2009 and found that a shocking 52 per cent had discrepancies between fish declared by vessels and fish weighed in the plant. The fraud is part of a wider trend of rampant overfishing and poor enforcement across the southern Pacific, says the ICIJ.

BLOOD FISH:
The real cost of prawn curry

3

When it emerged that Burmese nationals working on board Thai fishing boats were suffering brutal exploitation and appalling working conditions, it's unlikely many consumers gave it much thought. It is, after all, a long way from the Indian Ocean to supermarket aisles and restaurants in the West.

Blue Revolution

But the boats on which these abuses were occurring were found to be supplying 'trash fish'. This is used in the manufacture of fish feed given to prawns – or shrimp – cultivated in Thailand (and elsewhere) then exported

and consumed by diners across the world. Suddenly, the distance between our dinner plates and the Indian Ocean is not so great.

The revelations were just the latest in a series of disturbing exposés that have, in recent years, highlighted the often unsavoury nature of the global shrimp industry, which often brands itself as 'sustainable' and 'ethical'. But despite repeated campaigns to inform consumers about the often hidden environmental and social costs that lie behind the supply of prawns, the seafood treat remains highly popular.

Following the 'Blue Revolution' of the 1980s, which saw a huge expansion in aquaculture – and prawn farming in particular – in the coastal regions of Asia, Africa and Latin America, campaigners began to question the sustainability of shrimp, linking it to a number of serious environmental and social impacts.

Evidence emerged of the destruction of ecologically important mangrove forests to make way for prawn farms, leaving coastal communities increasingly vulnerable to rising sea levels and tsunamis. Shrimp cultivation ponds were also blamed for poisoning the water supplies of local people with harmful pesticides and antibiotics, and polluting agricultural land with salt water and waste.

Violence & intimidation

The arrival of industrial prawn farms – frequently producing shrimp for export markets – was also accompanied by violence and intimidation. Local people who protested against the building of prawn ponds in their backyards often found themselves targeted by hired thugs working on behalf of the shrimp industry. Researchers from the Environmental Justice Foundation (EJF) and other bodies uncovered a catalogue of human rights abuses connected to the prawn 'gold rush', including violent attacks, rape, arson and even murder.

A particularly disturbing investigation found how more than 150 people in Bangladesh – a major exporter of shrimp – had been killed in clashes relating to prawn farming. People like Zaheda Begum, leader of a women's association, reportedly shot dead by police who opened fire on a demonstration against the eviction of villagers to make way for prawn farms. Activists claimed at least 100 other people were wounded in the attack, the culmination of a campaign of intimidation and violence by criminal gangs – and police – acting on behalf of so-called 'shrimp barons'.

Investigations in 2003 uncovered how many Bangladeshi prawns linked to this chain of violence were finding their way into the UK for sale at ethnic food stores or for use in the catering industry.

Shockingly, very little appears to have changed. As fresh investigations in 2011 revealed, Bangladesh's shrimp-farming regions continue to be blighted by human rights abuses and environmental damage, according to campaigners, and Britain still imports many prawns from the region, despite calls for an embargo and repeated pledges to clean up the industry.

Food security

In Brazil, I witnessed first hand how our taste for prawns has had a big impact on poor coastal communities. In the village of Curral Velho, in Ceará state, residents complain bitterly that stocks of wild snails, mussels and crabs – all vital to local people's diets – have decreased since the arrival of industrial shrimp farms, and that salt water flooding from prawn ponds has destroyed their ability to cultivate crops. Similar stories are repeated elsewhere.

There is also evidence of mangrove and carnauba forests being felled to make way for shrimp farms. In some places, huge construction sites have replaced once intact ecosystems as the shrimp 'boom' took off. In Aracati, there is a site where a major canal is under construction to divert water from a nearby river to feed planned shrimp-producing ponds; ironically, many of the town's population already have no fresh water supply and have to rely on water being trucked in.

In Curral Velho, however, residents were determined to fight back. In an interview, community leader João Jaime Honório defiantly outlined their campaign of resistance:

'Ever since these shrimp farmers and their companies came to our area, we saw that they would not bring anything good for us, so from that moment on we have resisted this invasion […] I'll tell you that our families have been here for more than 100 years. We have lived here on our land for generations; it has been passed on from father to son. Everybody here works and survives because of the rivers, the shellfish and the sea. So we know that this shrimp farming is not a good thing for us. It brings only destruction.'

'Handcuffed & beaten'

A few months after this visit to Curral Velho, fishermen and community activists were injured during an attack by gunmen reportedly hired by a major shrimp-farming company. Residents say the

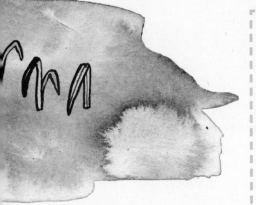

> **...salt water flooding from prawn ponds has destroyed their ability to cultivate crops.**

attack took place after they confronted employees over what they believed was the unlawful expansion of the farm's boundaries into nearby mangrove forests used by the community for fishing and docking boats. Despite constructive discussions with the farm owners, two fishermen were shot at later in the day by armed guards.

According to eyewitnesses, when a larger group of residents returned to demand an explanation for the violence, three gunmen from the farm opened fire indiscriminately – injuring six of the group, including three children. As some of the fishermen sought help from the nearby village, they were accosted by the gunmen, handcuffed and beaten, and threatened with death if they told anyone of the incident.

A LACK OF CERTIFICATION

Steps have been taken to curtail the activities of unscrupulous shrimp farmers across Brazil, yet the situation remains acute – as it does across swathes of the developing world. Recent years have seen increasing noise from within the industry about strict new certification schemes to ensure the sustainability of prawn production, and guarantee a better deal for all concerned. But many campaigners argue that the certification process itself has been weighted in favour of big business, and ignores many of the problems linked to industrial shrimp farms.

Labour conditions in the global fishing industry are largely absent from current seafood certification schemes – certainly none do much, if anything, to address the plight of the Burmese toiling on the fishing boats supplying 'trash fish' to the shrimp industry. For this reason alone, tropical prawns should be firmly blacklisted from all our shopping baskets.

WANT MORE INFO?
www.ejfoundation.org

FISHY BUSINESS:
The illegal shellfish trade that threatens our health

3

A favourite in soups, with pasta or served tapas-style, fresh clams are an increasingly popular, locally sourced seafood treat for millions of diners. But the illegal harvesting of clams, cockles and oysters – among other fish – for sale to restaurants and wholesalers threatens an outbreak of severe food poisoning.

Criminal gangs

An underground trade in shellfish is putting the health of consumers across Europe at risk with large volumes of potentially contaminated seafood entering the food chain. In the UK, highly organized gangs have been targeting shellfish stocks in the English counties of Sussex, Hampshire, Dorset, Merseyside, Lancashire, Cumbria and Teeside, among other areas. Parts of North Wales and Scotland have also been affected.

The criminal gangs target known shellfish beds by day or night, depending on the tides. Many arrive in transit vans or 4x4 vehicles and, using spades (or in some cases small boats fitted with dredging equipment), extract the lucrative molluscs before transferring them to chill boxes. From there, the shellfish are delivered to waiting merchants, or are offered for sale speculatively to traders, to restaurants or even via the internet. Some of the shellfish end up in markets for sale to the public, but most are thought to pass through processors or wholesalers who in turn sell to restaurants, pubs or other caterers, or export it abroad.

Legitimately gathered shellfish are subject to strict purification treatments to ensure they are fit for human consumption, but fish taken from prohibited or unclassified sources, or sold before being properly treated, put the public at risk of serious illnesses caused by the *E.coli*, norovirus or salmonella bugs.

Deadly outbreak

In 2011, a deadly *E.coli* outbreak – blamed first on cucumbers but later linked to German-grown bean sprouts – killed at least 22 people and poisoned more than 2,000 across Europe. Shellfish are frequently associated with instances of food poisoning, particularly when eaten raw or inadequately cooked, as they ingest viruses and bacteria that are potentially harmful to humans.

Although it is not illegal to harvest shellfish for personal consumption, strict food safety regulations make it an offence for molluscs to be gathered from unclassified fisheries and then sold on a commercial basis. European hygiene regulations insist waters used for commercial shellfish harvesting or cultivation are regularly tested for bacteria or virus levels, with different classification categories stipulating what processes harvested fish must go through before being safely consumed.

In 2011, research by the Food Standards Agency found traces of norovirus – or winter vomiting bug – in more than three-quarters of shellfish tested from UK beds, much of which is eliminated by treatment and cooking. In 2009, the Michelin-starred Fat Duck restaurant, owned by celebrity chef Heston Blumenthal, was forced to close after more than 450 people fell ill with norovirus. Raw oysters and clams were later identified by the Health Protection Agency as being the main source of the contamination.

The body says that at least 163 food-poisoning outbreaks recorded between 1992 and 2010 were linked to shellfish. It points to research published in the journal *Emerging Infectious Diseases* in 2005, which claimed that more than 77,000 cases of food-borne disease between 1996 and 2000 were linked to consumption of shellfish.

In 2011, research by the Food Standards Agency found traces of norovirus ... in more than three-quarters of shellfish tested from UK beds, much of which is eliminated by treatment and cooking.

WANT MORE INFO?
www.shellfish.org.uk
www.hpa.org.uk
www.gla.gov.uk

4 Dairy

INTRODUCTION

Millions of us were brought up believing that dairy cows spend their lives grazing in green fields and being gently led across the lane to the milking parlour twice a day. This may be true for some cows – at least for some of the time – but for many the reality is rather different. The dairy industry has become intensified. So-called 'zero-grazing' factory farms and 'mega dairies' have become the norm in the US, and this model is now spreading. Thousands of animals can be housed in a single facility, posing concerns over welfare. But alarm bells have also been rung about the wider environmental impacts of such developments – where does the feed come from? Where's the waste going to be disposed of? What's the impact on water supplies?

The Ecologist was one of the first to highlight the realities of intensive dairy production, as our articles here illustrate, and has done its best to assist those opposing the trend. Here, we champion those trying to do things differently and producing ethical milk – produced organically and biodynamically. But can this offer a viable alternative on a larger scale?

JUST HOW HEALTHY IS SOYA MILK?

4

It is an increasingly popular and heavily marketed alternative to dairy products, and a favourite for those trying to avoid unpleasant allergies. But, as *The Ecologist* magazine's acclaimed 'Behind the Label' series highlighted, this is not necessarily the full story.

Affecting fertility

For vegans, some dieters, some of those with allergies to cow's or goat's milk, or simply those with a taste for an alternative (and trendy) type of latte, soya milk must seem a godsend. And far from being an obscure drink found only on the dusty shelves of health food shops, soya milk is now a mainstream product consumed across large parts of the globe – indeed, in recent years food manufacturers have ploughed significant resources into marketing it as natural, healthy and tasty.

But the drink – and soya more widely – has been linked to a number of health concerns, including, disturbingly, decreased male fertility, as a major investigation by *The Observer*'s Antony Barnett first highlighted. He reported that academics, including Dr Lorraine Anderson from Belfast's Royal University Hospital, claim to have found correlations between 'slow moving sperm', which may hinder a couple's chances of

conceiving a baby, and the presence of isoflavones – sometimes known as plant-oestrogens because of their similarities with oestrogen, the female hormone – in seminal fluid.

Isoflavones are found in soya, and a man consuming large quantities of soya milk (or other soya products) may unwittingly be impacting upon his ability to help conceive a child, even with regular intercourse, some fertility experts have warned.

Lack of warnings

Pat Thomas, leading health journalist and former editor of *The Ecologist*, examined the evidence around the health implications of consuming soya as part of her 'Behind the Label' series, and highlighted further concerns around isoflavones: 'Isoflavones can disrupt hormone function in both men and women … high levels of circulating oestrogens are a risk for certain types of oestrogen-dependent cancers, for instance of the breast, ovaries and testicles,' she reported.

Thomas raised particular concerns relating to infants: 'Soya-based infant formula milk is widely available, often on the same shelves as varieties based on cow's milk, and is given to around 3 per cent of infants [in the UK]. This soya milk still contains isoflavone, exposure to which may impact on future fertility and reproductive development. The [UK] Government advises parents not to use soya-based formula without medical supervision, yet there is nothing to prevent parents using soya formula; neither are there any warnings on the packs.'

Cancer & allergies

Oestrogens in soya have also been implicated in thyroid cancer, and may cause an under-active thyroid, Thomas noted. There are links between babies fed soya formula and instances of autoimmune thyroid disease – a condition that can result in fatigue, exhaustion and depressive behaviour, among other symptoms.

Thomas also highlighted issues around soya-related allergens: '[...] Allergies to soya proteins – the symptoms of which include rashes, diarrhoea, vomiting, stomach cramps and breathing difficulties – are almost as common as those to milk.' In addition, she reported that, unknown to most consumers, 'soybeans, as found in nature, are not suitable for human consumption. Only after fermentation for some time, or extensive processing, including chemical extractions and high temperatures, are the beans – or the soya protein isolate – suitable for digestion.'

WANT MORE INFO?
www.theecologist.org

THE TRUTH ABOUT GOAT'S MILK

The popularity of goat's milk appears to be soaring, with 2012 the first year in which more than 2 million litres were estimated to be consumed in the UK. Around 70,000 animals are believed to be farmed for their milk in the UK; in the US, official statistics show the figure to be some 360,000. However, undercover investigations carried out by campaigners from the animal welfare group **VIVA!** may make you think twice before reaching for that carton of goat's milk, with allegations of zero grazing, mutilations and castration. *The Ecologist* spoke with **Justin Kerswell** from **VIVA!** about what they found during their research.

> **All the major problems inherent in the dairy farming of cows are applicable to goat farming, too. ... Most goat's milk sold in British supermarkets will come from factory farmed animals that never see a blade of grass.**

Ecologist: *Most people probably think goat's milk is a natural foodstuff produced from animals grazing in green fields. Why could that image be wrong?*

Justin Kerswell: All of the major problems inherent in the dairy farming of cows are applicable to goat farming, too. You have to take a baby away from its mother so you can take her milk. Males can't be milked, so are either killed at birth, often by having their heads smashed against hard surfaces, or are mostly sold for halal slaughter at between 5 weeks and 11 months old. Also, it's sadly ironic that we are so worried about the looming threat of zero

> **The modern dairy goat industry is underpinned and only possible by the mutilation of baby animals at just a day or two old. Usually without anaesthetic, they are ear-tagged and most have the tips of their horns burnt off.**

grazing for dairy cows in Britain when it is already common practice for dairy goats here, with only one large producer allowing their goats to graze. Most goat's milk sold in UK supermarkets will come from factory farmed-animals that never see a blade of grass.

Ecologist: *Viva's filming at UK goat farms was undeniably shocking. But do you think the conditions uncovered were isolated examples of bad husbandry, or is goat farming inherently cruel?*

JK: The modern dairy goat industry is underpinned, and only possible, by the mutilation of baby animals at just a day or two old. Usually without anaesthetic, they are ear-tagged and most have the tips of their horns burnt off. Males suffer further with a method of castration that can cause significant short- and long-term pain. Most of these highly intelligent and inquisitive animals spend most of their lives in intensive sheds. The cruelty is sadly routine.

Ecologist: *Who, in Viva's opinion, needs to be held responsible for the poor conditions and procedures at the goat farms documented, e.g. the farmers, vets, retailers …?*

JK: One of the farms we filmed at burned the horn buds off hundreds of young goats without anaesthetic. This procedure should be done by a vet and it wasn't. The explanation was that it would cost too much money for farms with large numbers of animals. You have to wonder where else this is happening and why the authorities seemingly turn a blind eye to potential widespread illegality. We would like to see the Government ban mutilations, but the truth is that factory farming couldn't exist without them.

WANT MORE INFO?
www.milkmyths.org.uk
www.viva.org.uk

SOUR MILK:
Inside the US 'mega-dairy' industry

4

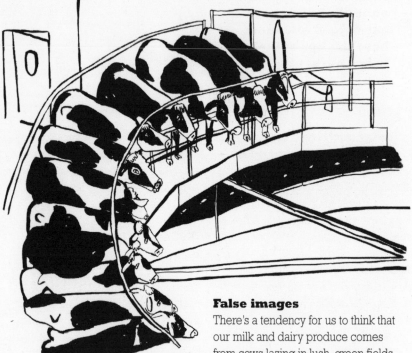

False images

There's a tendency for us to think that our milk and dairy produce comes from cows lazing in lush, green fields in a bucolic countryside, with farmers herding their animals up at regular intervals for a stroll to the milking parlour. But nothing could be further from the truth, with many dairy farms now effectively operating as intensive factory units with apparently little regard for animal welfare or the impacts on people or the environment.

Although controversial plans for the UK's first 'mega dairy' – containing up to 4,000 cows – in Lincolnshire were

Dairy farms are becoming increasingly intensive with more and more cows being housed in battery-style 'zero-grazing' units. But it's not just animal welfare that suffers when farms expand in size, as a groundbreaking investigation by *The Ecologist* and campaigners from the World Society for the Protection of Animals (WSPA) found.

recently defeated after a groundswell of public anger at the proposals, the spectre of giant milk-producing farms springing up elsewhere across the country remains real. Similar schemes are currently being proposed elsewhere in the UK and critics warn the trend is only likely to increase as pressure on farmers to produce more milk for less money continues to grow.

As part of a major campaign against the intensification of dairy farming, *The Ecologist* teamed up with researchers from the World Society for the Protection of Animals (WSPA) to visit California in the US, where 'mega dairies' are firmly established, to try to better understand just what the impact of their arrival has been. What we uncovered was a disturbing pattern of factory farming, conflict, intimidation, the rampant use of chemicals, pollution and evidence that small-scale farmers are being driven out of business.

Investigative reporter Jim Wickens travelled to California's Central Valley – an arid plain that stretches down the state, wedged in between the Sierra Foothills and the Californian coast – where some of the world's largest mega dairies are sited. He found that in one county alone, Tulare, there are nearly a million cows producing in excess of a billion dollars worth of milk each year ...

Factory or farm?

For a first-time visitor, the sight and scale of a mega dairy is overwhelming – enormous, open-air sheds, mountains of feed, million-gallon pools of slurry and thousands upon thousands of listless cows. Granted access by disgruntled dairy employees, we were able to observe a mega dairy in operation. More akin to a factory production line than a farm, long lines of cows could be seen stumbling over outstretched udders as they were driven back and forth to the robotic-like, rotary-milking parlours.

It is a continual daily cycle that stops only when the milk output begins to tail off, and the animals are either re-impregnated or sent off to slaughter, burnt out and discarded after only a few years of life on the factory floor. Animals in US mega dairies will never see a patch of grass in their life, and the only respite comes from shade in the dusty, open-air lots where they wait between milking. Even here the animals will not get a chance to really rest; high-milk yielding cows suffer from chronic 'negative energy balance', where the cow uses more energy in making milk than she can physically take in by eating, losing body condition as a result.

The Holstein is the favoured breed of choice for many mega dairies. Their towering bony frames contrast wildly with bulging vein-filled udders swinging underneath them ... Milk produced by them is of a lower quality with a higher pus content in the milk than that produced by other cow breeds, but what these freakishly bred animals lack in quality, they make up for in quantity: milked three times a day and propped up with growth hormones to boost milk production, and antibiotics to stave off frequent infections, milk output in the Holstein has doubled in the last 40 years alone.

Flies & nitrates

And it is not just animals that suffer. Tom Frantz, a retired school teacher interviewed as part of the investigation, said. 'Until 1996, there weren't any dairies near me, then we got the first mega dairy situated close to here, followed by several others. Within a couple of years at the local school we had two big problems that have never existed before... the school was invaded by hordes of flies, nasty biting flies, clogging the water coolers and forcing the teachers to hang fly strips in the middle of each classroom. It changed things, changed the atmosphere of the school. Then nitrates in the water showed up. The school had always used water from its own well in the past, but suddenly the nitrate level doubled, then tripled, making it unsafe to drink.'

Frantz had put together a community action group in an attempt to stop further dairies from encroaching on communities. His campaigning came at a cost, however; he has been threatened and now lives with restraining orders in place against overly aggressive dairymen living nearby.

So-called mega dairies pose a different type of threat to the Central Valley, too, with farms producing high quantities of gases leading to smog and particulate pollution. According to the American Lung Association, pollution from industrial agriculture operations 'poses a significant health threat for some of the most vulnerable people in our community. Children, adolescents, seniors, people with asthma and chronic lung diseases, people with chronic heart disease and diabetics are most at risk'.

Pesticides

The impact of pesticide usage in the dairy sector was also highlighted. Teresa DeAnda, a mother of seven and campaigner on the issue, says: 'I was always interested in reading the news about air pollution and I knew air quality was getting worse. I knew that was all bad, then I read an article that they wanted to put in a dairy of 5,000 cows in Kings county nearby and I was so upset, and I said "oh my gosh I got to go over there"'.

With the assistance of the Council for Race Poverty and the Environment, Teresa began to work full time on pesticide issues and air quality – fighting against pollution on behalf of the voiceless Hispanic populations living nearby. The more she looked into the problem, the more frustrated she became. 'There have been studies done looking at why polluting industries move to certain areas,' she says. 'These industries actually look for neighbours who are Hispanic, low income, poor, of colour and are Catholic. And it makes me so angry, big dairies pollute until water boards crack down on them, so then the dairies sell up and move here ... where nobody complains.'

Driving along the highway, Teresa waves at countless gangs of migrant workers as they work in lines, silently packing grapes. A few miles out of town, fruit fields give way to vast fields of corn and alfalfa, crops all grown to feed the cows in the mega dairies. We are en route to meet Jorge, a Salvadorian worker whose family has experienced the impact of pesticides used to grow crops for cattle. Teresa explains that Jorge is an exception to the rule, usually

people here don't want to speak out as 'they could lose their jobs and their homes … they're scared'.

Jorge complains bitterly about the pesticides used to grow cattle feed: 'I used to have cows, but they all died … I had canaries they all died … I had goats, but I sold them because they were dying too; they had stomach problems and the babies were also dying.' Jorge guides us around his smallholding. He has a few horses left, but for the most part the stables are empty, weeds sprouting from the dust. He points to the few remaining fruit trees his family planted, bare stems save for a few shrivelled brown leaves at the end of each branch. 'When I came here my financial situation was good and I was comfortable … it [pesticide spraying] has had a very bad impact because the children became ill, the animals are dying, I am ill,' he says.

DECLINING DAIRIES

Not all Californian dairies are operating on such a large scale. Paul Bianci tends a small herd of Jersey cows, which spend much of the year grazing on pasture in the rolling hills of Northern California. In scale and sight, Paul's farm resembles a British farm, and is perhaps a decent barometer of what mega dairies might mean for British farmers if they come to Britain. 'We just can't compete with them ... they just put the little people out of business,' he told us. We heard similar complaints from other small farmers we met – that economies of scale make it virtually impossible to compete with mega dairies who are milking herds of cows up to a hundred times bigger than smaller family farms, driving down milk prices and forcing family farmers to sell up.

Albert Strauss, who runs a successful organic dairy, has pioneered an alternative system to provide California with a more sustainable milk supply: 'We lose 55 of our dairies each year, and in the last 40 years in our district alone we have gone from 120 dairies to 23 ... so it's a bit drastic. Mega dairies are continuing the trend away from sustainable farming, and it's happening because mega dairies dominate because they are the biggest agricultural commodity in the USA, and when you have big dairies controlling most of the milk supply, you have a lot more political power.'

The problem isn't just confined to California – according to the US Department of Agriculture (USDA) statistics, 33,000 dairies disappeared

nationwide between 1997 and 2002. Our last day in California is spent at Turlock County Fair, a 'mom and pop type' family affair where dairy farmers from the Central Valley help their children to show prize animals in front of the judges. Behind the showground, children are busy grooming the prize cows that will soon be led out into the arena, while parents sit and chat over beers nearby. It is a timeless scene from small–town America, but despite the friendly feel of the place, few want to talk to journalists asking questions about mega dairies; we are met with a wall of silence, people too scared to be seen talking about their problems.

Finally we meet Paul Clarent, a Stetson-wearing, unapologetic mega-dairy owner, who flatly rejects the concerns of smaller farmers we had spoken with during the week: 'You've got to expand to compete with the big guys ... that's just business and that's life, it's not fair all the time,' he said. As we are preparing to leave the fair, an elderly farmer beckons us over away from the crowds and offers up a different reality. 'Listen, we run a dairy and you know we will probably go out of business in the next two or three years. We are simply not big enough to compete with the big dairies... my grandparents, my parents, my wife and I did this to pass on to our kids and now it's going to die with my daughter's generation. It's pretty sad,' he said.

WANT MORE INFO?
www.wspa.org.uk

BIODYNAMIC COWS:
The micro-dairy challenging conventional milk production

4

Despite the growing intensification of the dairy sector, it is still possible to produce milk, cheese and other dairy goods sustainably and humanely, as one pioneering farm in the south of England shows.

A shopful of real food

The Plaw Hatch farm shop, nestling in the beautiful countryside of the Ashdown Forest in Sussex, is how shops once were, and probably should be again in the future.

Minimal gimmickry – no flashy signage, overpowering advertising, or misleading '2 for 1' offers. Lots of daylight, sacks and pallets, boxes, authentic smells. And – most importantly – piles of real food, unburdened, in the main, by excessive packaging or fanfare.

Food on sale includes fruit and vegetables, groceries, fresh bread, cakes, meat, oils, juices, wine and cider, cheeses, milk and yogurt. Virtually everything is organic and much is biodynamic. A significant proportion is produced by the very farm upon which the shop sits, or by its sister enterprise, Tablehurst, in nearby Forest Row.

Both are community farms and together form the 'Tablehurst and Plaw Hatch Community Farm Industrial and Provident Society', which in effect means they are owned and operated democratically by upwards of some 500 local people – plus outside supporters – who are each shareholders. (Each farm is actually a limited company employing dedicated staff who are responsible for the day-to-day farming activities; a separate committee oversees the longer term development of the ventures.)

Business manager John Twyford and dairy herdsman Tom Ventham (who has since left) explained how the majority of the food produced is sold direct to the public from the farm gate. Plaw Hatch focuses on horticulture and a dairy enterprise that produces raw milk, yogurt, cream and cheese.

'Self-sustaining'

The dairy herd comprises 40 Meuse-Rhine-Issel (MRI) cows, managed to strict biodynamic principles. The Biodynamic Agricultural Association (BDA), an industry trade body, summarizes this thus: 'A biodynamic farm functions as a strong, self-sustaining and vibrant single organism that recognizes and respects the basic principles at work in nature. It is a complete system in which all the different components of the farm are seen as parts of a greater whole. With farm animals at the centre, a self-sustaining, balanced and harmonious environment is the result.'

Biodynamic agriculture is based on the teachings of the philosopher Rudolf Steiner, who, in the 1920s, began to outline his vision for a more holistic form of farming in a direct challenge to what he saw as the alarming degradation of soil quality across Europe because of overuse of inorganic fertilizers and pesticides.

In common with organic agriculture, biodynamic farming practices strictly limit the use of pesticides and other chemicals, and minimize the administration of antibiotics to livestock. But central to the biodynamic approach is the application of homeopathic-style preparations to compost and soil to improve the microbiological life of the soil and stimulate fertility. John and Tom confirmed that such preparations are used at Plaw Hatch. They admitted there's little scientific research to

illustrate the benefits, but, in keeping with the wider biodynamic philosophy, state that 'something bigger' is definitely going on.

A biodynamic calendar, taking into account the movements of the earth, sun, moon, planets and constellations, is also often used. These two 'tools' underpin the system and, say its advocates, ensure that food produced using biodynamic methods has optimum goodness and vitality while imposing a lighter footprint on the land.

Animal welfare

In common with other biodynamic dairy farms, the Plaw Hatch cows are not de-horned. This is because horns are seen as an intrinsic part of the animal's 'whole' being, and biodynamic thinking places the cow at the very centre of the wider farm 'organism', in both a practical and a spiritual sense.

The confined conditions found in some larger, conventional farms (one reason that most cows have their horns removed) are not an issue at Plaw Hatch – although the herd spends some time in the large barn in winter, the cows are about as free range as can be. This is a far cry from the trend of 'upscaling' dairy farms towards the intensive US model, where thousands of animals are housed in feedlots (with feed brought to them, rather than being able to graze).

Proposed 'mega dairies' such as this in the UK have attracted huge controversy because of concerns over poor welfare conditions and environmental impacts. Plaw Hatch should be regarded as an antidote to such developments – each cow has a name! – and those involved in farming the creatures do so, it appears, with a degree of respect and dedication not always present elsewhere.

All this risks sounding idyllic, and in many ways it is, especially when combined with the farm's policy of transparency and inclusiveness – Plaw Hatch is 'open', meaning that anyone is welcome to turn up and have a look around, and people of all ages and from all walks of life are encouraged to become involved, including those with special needs.

The age of cheap food

But ensuring farmland remains productive and sustainably managed is not always easy; neither is the challenge of remaining commercially viable in the age of cheap food and competition from conventional supermarkets.

Those running Plaw Hatch admit the food they produce and subsequently sell is not the cheapest – 'more than Sainsbury's, but not more than Waitrose', according to John – but say this reflects the true cost of ethical food production. The shop serves a quite affluent area, but still attracts 'normal' families for whom food is really important. 'People do [come here] to do bulk, staple shopping – potatoes, broccoli, tomatoes,' John says.

The farm currently has up to 12 people living on site – three or four staff members and five or six student volunteers – to manage operations day to day, helped out by volunteers. In 2011, the turnover was some £670,000, with £240,000 of that generated by Plaw Hatch's own food. In 2012, this increased to £812,000, with a healthy profit of £48,000. This is a far cry from recent years when the venture was struggling to turn over much at all, let alone make a profit.

Although biodynamic farming by nature is focused on the local ('We don't want to feed the world, just our community,' says John), making the approach work on a truly commercial scale is largely untested. Plaw Hatch therefore offers an inspiring and, based on present figures, potentially viable example of ethical farming.

WANT MORE INFO?
www.tablehurstand
plawhatch.co.uk

5 Grocery

INTRODUCTION

Few would imagine that tinned tomatoes could pose consumers with any ethical problems. But, as *The Ecologist*'s alarming investigation into the Italian tomato trade revealed, things are not that simple. We uncovered how thousands of African migrants endure squalid, slave-like conditions in order to scratch a living harvesting tomatoes destined for the UK and other European markets.

Perhaps even more shocking than the scandal itself is the apparent culture of impunity around the issue, with farmers, producers and retailers apparently ignoring the rampant exploitation and abuse in their supply chains. Unfortunately, as the pieces included here highlight, human rights abuses, environmental problems and widespread impunity appear to blight so many of the everyday staples we all take for granted.

Although in many cases the root problems are complex (and solutions hard to implement), there's now almost universal consensus that manufacturers and retailers should be forced to do much, much more to ensure their supply chains are 'clean'.

TAINTED TOMATOES

5

They are among our most popular and versatile foods. But across Italy an invisible army of migrant workers harvesting tomatoes endure poverty wages and squalid living conditions that medical charities have described as 'hell'.

'Tomato slaves'

In the parched countryside outside the town of Venosa, southern Italy, along a rough track 15 minutes' drive from the nearest road, is a series of ruined farmhouses. Overgrown and run-down, the brickwork crumbling, and surrounded by the detritus of poverty – rubbish, abandoned water butts, washing draped out of windows, dogs roaming – it's difficult to believe anyone lives here. The slums are in fact home to several hundred migrant workers about to harvest the region's abundant tomato crop. Every August, thousands of itinerants, mostly from Africa, descend on southern Italy to scratch a living picking tomatoes that will

be processed and exported across Europe to be sold in tins, or as pastes, purées or passatas, or used in other food products.

But this lucrative trade is blighted by exploitation and abuse. Workers are forced to toil for up to 14 hours a day in harsh conditions for meagre wages, frequently under the control of gangmasters who can make excessive deductions or charge inflated rates for transport, accommodation, food and other 'services'. Those complaining face violence and intimidation.

Workers frequently live in appalling squalor: home is often a derelict building without power or any form of sanitation. As many as 30 people can be crammed into a single, filthy, one-floor house. Health care is virtually non-existent and contact with the outside world is minimal. So bad are the living and working conditions that campaigners have dubbed the migrants 'Europe's tomato slaves'.

Trapped in poverty

Most seek out the precarious employment in order to send money back home, but find themselves caught in a brutal spiral of poverty and exploitation. Unable to save sufficiently to transfer money – or pay for a flight out of Europe – they become trapped and are forced to seek out similarly low-paid work harvesting oranges, lemons, olives or strawberries in order to survive.

Human rights groups say as many as 50,000 migrant workers are toiling in the agricultural regions of Puglia, Basilicata and Campania, among others. The figure could be higher as many migrants are in the country illegally. Médecins Sans Frontières (MSF) – more usually associated with providing medical aid in conflict zones – has sent mobile clinics to treat migrants in some areas, and described the workers' experiences as 'hell'.

Suffering & squalor

In the fields outside Venosa, people are reluctant to talk to journalists. There had been rumours of television cameras coming, and – in a clear sign many were in Italy without visas – fears that the 'authorities' could be conducting inspections. One man refuses to look up from gutting the carcass of an unidentifiable animal hanging from the shack's roof.

Further down the track is another, almost identical, building. A dozen young African men are gathered around. These guys are happier to talk: this house is 'home' to 15 migrants, mostly from West Africa – countries such

FROM FIELD TO SUPERMARKET

Tomatoes are big business in Italy: the country produces up to 4 million tonnes each year with as much as 90 per cent destined for processing. Italian tinned tomato exports were estimated to be worth more than $900 million in 2008. The country is responsible for around 75 per cent of the world's canned tomato exports. The UK is the largest importer of tinned tomatoes in the world – with more than 80 per cent of its processed tomato products coming from Italy. The trade is dominated by a handful of companies who supply major UK supermarket outlets and wholesalers. If you've ever eaten a tinned tomato, or a tomato pizza topping, chances are it came from Italy.

the coming days, he expects to spend between 10 and 12 hours a day in the exposed tomato fields, picking by hand; bending, plucking and carrying the filled crates. The work is arduous, repetitive and hot. The temperature can reach 40 degrees C (104°F).

as Ivory Coast, Burkina Faso and Ghana. There's no running water or electricity. The men appear to sleep communally on mattresses spread out across the stone floor. Their cooking, washing and toilet facilities are outdoors. The tomato harvest begins in late August in Basilicata; when it does, these men will be joined by up to 15 more workers. The house will be so overcrowded that some will have to sleep outside.

The men are here for one thing: to work. Some had been in Italy for several months, some for several years. Most had no idea of when – or how – they'll return home. Asked whether this is what he expected to find when he set out for Italy, one worker, Joseph, from Ghana, tells me: 'It's not what we expected to find that matters, but what we found.'

Daniel, from Burkina Faso, tells me that once the harvest gets underway in

Gangmasters

Contracts are non-existent for most tomato pickers. The migrants are paid on a piece-rate system based on the amount of tomatoes harvested. Although it can vary, Daniel and Joseph expect to earn 20–30 euros (£17–26) per day – the current going 'rate' – depending on the number of crates picked. The crates are heavy, holding as many as 35 kg (75 lbs) of tomatoes when full.

'But there's only enough work for three days [per week],' Daniel says. 'The other days are spent here.' This means, in practice, that some workers here could earn no more than 51 euros (£45) per week. And that's before a

gangmaster has taken his cut or
workers have paid for essential items.

In common with horticultural
operations across Europe and in the
US, gangmasters are central to Italy's
tomato harvest. They broker deals
with farmers and producers, and
supply the workforce, as well as
providing transport and organizing
accommodation, food, water and other
essentials for the workers.

Some deduct money from wages
upfront for workers' food, accommodation
and transport. Others charge for these
essentials after the workers have been
paid. Other 'services' and supplies
must also be paid for – charging

a mobile phone, organizing
clean drinking water,
supplying a bike – with
many enterprising gangmasters
ensuring they take a cut on each sale.

An African gangmaster is present
at our visit. He's indistinguishable apart
from being marginally better dressed
than his peers, and being one of few
who say they've managed to return
home – in his case, Ivory Coast –
since arriving in Italy. His presence
means these workers are nervous
about openly discussing financial
details, although one complains that
'too much money' is sometimes
charged for basic items.

Intimidation & violence

Relations between gangmasters and workers frequently break down as resentment over exploitative practices spills over. An investigation by *L'espresso* magazine in 2006 revealed how migrant workers harvesting tomatoes in Puglia were frequently threatened, beaten up and racially abused by gangmasters and farm owners. In one incident, a Romanian worker was allegedly savagely beaten before being left to die – he was later secretly fed by fellow workers and taken to hospital where, after an operation, he was handed over to police for deportation.

He was lucky to have received treatment. MSF has reported that many migrant workers employed in southern Italy's tomato and citrus fruit harvests have been turned away from hospitals, and that others, without permission to be in Italy, have been too afraid to access medical attention.

Gervasio Ungolo, from Osservatorio Migranti, which works to improve conditions for migrant communities, says that conditions are so poor and the future so bleak that many migrants simply despair. 'They reach the bottom of the scale, the bottom of the barrel,' he says, 'they lose all self respect.'

Keeping costs down

Few tomato farmers admit to employing migrants despite it being an 'open secret'. One grower, however, acknowledges that the practice is common, particularly

> **[Médecins Sans Frontières] has reported that many migrant workers employed in southern Italy's tomato and citrus fruit harvests have been turned away from hospitals, and that others, without permission to be in Italy, have been too afraid to access medical attention.**

when weather conditions are poor and machines (increasingly used by larger farms to harvest mechanically) cannot operate.

The farmer, Giovanni Lagana, based near the town of Lavello, tells me that foreign workers have been employed during the Basilicata tomato harvest for years. 'Twenty years ago, in the beginning, they were from North Africa, now it's Central or Western Africa,' he says. 'Tunisian students came to train and learn the harvest.'

He says the migrant workers he uses are 80 per cent African, 20 per cent Eastern European – Italians apparently don't want to do the work – and that all are supplied by a gangmaster. 'It's necessary [to use gangmasters] so I don't have to talk to 40 people, just one, to arrange the work. They say "how many workers do you need?", we negotiate the price for a box, it's a guarantee for the workers and farmers – they take care of everything.'

Lagana, who cultivates up to 900 tonnes of tomatoes each season, some of which are supplied to major processing companies for export and sale as tinned tomatoes overseas, says there is an economic imperative to keep costs, including labour costs, down: 'The price we have now in 2011 [for tomatoes] is the same as 30 years ago, but the [production] costs have risen.'

The farmer says tomato growers are under acute pressure as plants, irrigation systems, fertilizers, pesticides and the harvest all have to be paid for upfront, and that the prices paid by the food industry are too low.

CULTURE OF IMPUNITY

Human rights groups and unions believe that many growers simply turn a blind eye to exploitation: 'Farmers? They don't care, they know about the inhumane conditions,' says Vincenzo Esposito, from the trade union Flai-Cgil. Esposito says there are two principal problems – the number of workers, and the payment system: 'There's too many workers, too many people, immigrants from elsewhere coming here, yet they cannot always get work here,' he says. 'Every year the Basilicata region deals with an emergency situation with the arrival of hundreds of workers. The situation in Puglia is worse, and the gangmasters are more aggressive.'

Flai-Cgil is calling for an industry-wide protocol, akin to a certification scheme, to be adopted by national tomato producers, in order to agree minimum standards and an ethical code. Esposito hopes their efforts will prove successful – soon: 'We've got immigrants living without water, without electricity… they are treated like animals.'

www.flai.it

DRIZZLE WITH CARE

Olive oil has become the oil of choice for foodies across the Western world. And despite revelations that some within the industry have been defrauding consumers with cheap substitutes and adulteration, the impact of production on the environment has largely been ignored.

Widespread fraud

Recent years have seen kitchen store cupboard favourite olive oil hitting the headlines for the wrong reasons – including the widely reported claims that some leading Italian producers had been contaminating higher quality Italian oil with cheaper, less wholesome oils originating elsewhere in southern Europe and even North Africa.

The dark secrets of the olive oil industry were last year laid bare in disturbing detail in a major investigative book, *Extra Virginity: The Sublime and Scandalous World of Olive Oil*, by US writer Tom Mueller. The book highlighted just how widespread fraudulent practices in the sector have become and, in short, informed us that the 'extra virgin' label so commonly attached to the oils we buy may not be quite so virgin after all.

But although the focus of recent attention has been on the scams and deep deception of millions of consumers,

what about another, perhaps even less visible, aspect of the oil's production, that of its environmental impact? In a scathing critique of the production processes associated with conventional olive oil, *The Ecologist*'s Laura Sevier highlighted even more worrying reasons that shoppers might want to think twice before reaching for the bottle…

Environmental hazard

Olive oil has joined the ranks of tomato ketchup, mayonnaise and marmalade to become a national staple. Demand has soared. But while we may be benefiting from more and cheaper olive oil in our diets, there is a price to pay. Growing olives on an industrial scale is an environmental hazard – with impacts on the soil, water supply and wildlife.

Read the label of most bottles of olive oil and the chances are the olives it came from were grown in the EU. Olives are one of the EU's most abundant crops: Italy, Spain, Portugal and Greece are the largest producers; they dominate the global olive market. But not all olives are grown in the same way. Industrial olive farms grow their olive trees, planted at high densities, in massive irrigated orchards on lowland plains. The olives are harvested by machines that clamp around the tree's trunk and shake it until the olives fall to the ground.

Oil is then extracted by industrial-scale centrifuge, often at high temperatures. In contrast, small, traditional farms are often ancient, their trees typically planted on upland terraces. The farmers manage their groves with few or no agrochemicals, less water and less machinery. Olives are picked off the ground by hand and the oil extracted by grinding the olives in a millstone and press. Demand for cheap, mass-produced oil is making it a struggle for the smaller, traditional farms to be economically viable, however.

Soil erosion

Intensive olive farming is a major cause of one of the biggest environmental problems affecting the EU: widespread soil erosion and desertification in Spain, Greece, Italy and Portugal.

In 2001, the European Commission ordered an independent study into the environmental impact of olive farming across the EU. The report concluded: 'Soil erosion is probably the most serious environmental problem associated with olive farming. Inappropriate weed-control and soil-management practices, combined with the inherently high risk of erosion in many olive-farming areas, is leading to desertification on a wide scale in some of the main producing regions, as well as considerable run-off of soils and agrochemicals into water bodies.'

'Anywhere in the main olive-producing areas you can see tremendous soil erosion,' says Guy Beaufoy, a consultant on agricultural and environmental policies in Europe. 'It's an environmental catastrophe.'

It is starting to be tackled through cross-compliance: that is, by complying with environmental legislation plus some soil protection measures – not ploughing up and down a steep slope, for example, and maintaining a proportion of ground cover, such as grass, to protect the soil between olive rows on slopes. Policing it is a problem, though, and there is too little checking to see whether farmers are complying with the rules.

Eroded soils and farmland chemicals are among the principal pollutants of surface waters in Mediterranean regions.

Water shortages

Compared to horticulture or arable crops, olive production does require lower quantities of water. Irrigated olives are very efficient, but the trouble is there are hundreds of thousands of hectares of olives being irrigated – far more than lettuce or tomatoes – and that area is growing, so the magnitude of the impact is significant.

The regions affected by the expansion of irrigated olive plantations often have serious water shortage problems. For example, in Puglia (Italy), Crete and Jaén (Spain), irrigated olive plantations have continued to expand even though ground waters are already severely depleted.

Celsa Peiteado, WWF Spain's agricultural and rural development policy officer, says this is the fourth consecutive year that Spain has suffered a drought. 'WWF is very concerned about the massive transformation of the vineyards and olive groves, traditionally dry crops, into irrigated crops, as has been occurring for the last few years,' she says.

Industrial olive oil production involves a dramatic change in land use, from extensive cereal production or mixed cultivation, or even natural woodland or scrub (all with high biodiversity value), to a more intensive, irrigated and mechanized means of producing olives. This – 'above all else' – is the concern of WWF Spain's Ana Carricondo: 'Techniques that are used by intensive farms to increase production – especially frequent tillage and heavy pesticide use – result in a considerable reduction in the diversity and total numbers of flora and fauna,' she says.

WANT MORE INFO?
www.wwf.org.uk

A BETTER WAY?

Spain is the world's leading olive oil producer, its 300 million trees contributing almost one million tonnes of oil each year to the world market. Andalucía itself accounts for 80 per cent of Spanish olive oil. It's not all herbicides, pesticides and mechanical harvesters, however; there are producers who stick to traditional methods and grow their olives organically.

'Organic production of olives can be almost as great as industrial production, if special attention is given to each stage of the process,' says Andalucían producer Paco Núñez de Prado. 'The only difference is that the organic process will have around 20 per cent higher costs.' The Núñez de Prado family has been producing olive oil on their family estate in the Baena region for 200 years.

After picking, the olives are swiftly stone-crushed, using traditional mills introduced by the Romans. Stone milling ensures the olives remain cool when crushed; the oil obtained this way is low in acidity. The pulp and vegetable water are used to make biological compost. The groves aren't ploughed; instead a covering of vegetation is permanently maintained that protects the soil from the direct rays of the sun, maintains the humidity of the ground and prevents soil erosion, even during torrential downpours. The difference in the landscape is striking. The ground under the estate's trees grows a healthy, lush green, instead of the bare red earth of surrounding groves.

The groves are irrigated via an underground irrigation system – a better use of water, as less is wasted through evaporation – from a regulated reservoir that permits certain limits of water depending on the rainfall that year.

BAD EGGS:
WHY THERE'S SOMETHING ROTTEN DOWN ON THE FARM

It is estimated that up to 40 million day-old male chicks are killed in Britain each year. Secret filming in hatcheries has revealed how many of these birds are either gassed or thrown into electric mincers alive. And this is just one aspect of an industry riddled with welfare problems, says VIVA!'s **Justin Kerswell**, who spoke to *The Ecologist*.

Ecologist: *Viva! has done a lot of work over the years highlighting problems in egg production. Could you outline for us the principal welfare factors consumers should be aware of?*

Justin Kerswell: Eggs are big business in the UK. I think most consumers would be surprised at how big and how intensive the British egg industry actually is. Just over 11.5 billion eggs are consumed in the UK every year (around 32 million a day). Over 85 per cent of these are produced domestically, with the nation's 29 million laying hens each laying an average of 314 eggs per year – nearly one per day. [...]

Chickens raised for meat are of a different breed from egg-laying chickens. Males of the egg-laying breed do not gain weight fast enough to be raised profitably for meat. Very few of them are needed for breeding future generations of laying hens, so most are killed shortly after birth. It is estimated that 30–40 million day-old male chicks are killed in Britain each year [...], either gassed or thrown into electric mincers alive. This is entirely legal. The truth is that the egg industry simply couldn't exist without this horrendous waste of life.

> ... free-range egg farming [in Britain] is now such big business there is often little to differentiate it from factory farming, with thousands of hens housed in massive industrial sheds.

Ecologist: *So-called battery cages for egg-laying hens have recently been outlawed in the UK. Doesn't this mean that eating eggs is now OK?*

JK: In a word, no. While battery cages have been outlawed in Britain, they have just been replaced by another cage – albeit a slightly bigger one.

These new 'enriched' cages must provide 750 cm^2 of space per hen as well as limited perching, nesting and scratching facilities. This meagre extra space requirement, less than a postcard-sized space per bird, means hens will still be severely restricted and unable to stretch or flap their wings. Hens will also still be painfully debeaked to try to stop the very pecking and cannibalistic behaviours that unnatural environments such as these encourage.

Most birds in enriched cages will still spend a significant proportion of their time standing on sloping wire mesh floors with little room to move around, and they will all still be denied fresh air and sunshine. For these reasons, all the major animal welfare organizations in the EU continue to push for a complete ban on cages – conventional and enriched.

Ecologist: *Are there any types of eggs available in typical shops and supermarkets that are fine to eat? And are other foodstuffs containing eggs likely to be 'cruelty-free'?*

JK: No, and that's why we advocate a vegan diet. While there are varying farm standards, all eggs and products with eggs in them share the same fundamental issues. [...] Although

hailed as one of the great welfare success stories of the past 20 years, [...] free-range egg farming [in Britain] is now such big business there is often little to differentiate it from factory farming, with thousands of hens housed in massive industrial sheds. Although free-range birds have access to the outside, that doesn't mean that they go outside. Our investigations have shown that many never will...

RAISING GOOD EGGS

Although concerned consumers can insist on organic, free range, locally produced eggs, the egg industry remains inherently wasteful, according to animal welfare campaigners and organizations like Viva!. Perhaps, then, the only way of ensuring the ethical status of our eggs if we do choose to eat them – and eating them in complete confidence – is by raising hens ourselves. The practice has become increasingly popular in recent years, with home-grown eggs offering a cheap and guilt-free alternative.

For more information, see: 'The A–Z of Chicken Keeping' at www.theecologist.org

WANT MORE INFO?
www.viva.org.uk

REAL BREAD

Recent years have seen a growing backlash against bland, industrially produced breads. But 'real' bread is neither expensive nor complicated to make yourself, as **Emmanuel Hadjiandreou**, celebrated baker and author of **HOW TO MAKE BREAD**, tells *The Ecologist*.

Ecologist: *You specialize in artisanal breads and baking – why are you so passionate about 'real' bread and in getting people interested in baking?*

Emmanuel Hadjiandreou: Through my years of baking and running bakeries, I have enormous pleasure in introducing enthusiastic and passionate people to my world of bread and inspiring them to enjoy the rewards of making loaves to be proud of. I believe that everyone can make a loaf of bread, and with practice, it can be a great loaf.

> **When you make real bread, you rely on the yeast to make the bread rise and to encourage fermentation to take place, which produces flavour and texture.**

Ecologist: *What's the basic differences – in terms of ingredients and processes – between 'real' bread and the cheap mass-produced loaves we are probably all more familiar with?*

EH: In real bread, the ingredients are flour, water, yeast and salt. Very simple and straightforward. In mass-produced breads, the ingredients used tend to be a much longer list with processing aids and artificial additives. When you make real bread, you rely on the yeast to make the bread rise and to encourage fermentation to take place, which produces flavour and texture. In mass-produced bread, there is hardly any fermentation and there are ingredients used to imitate the flavour you get from the long fermentation you have when making real bread. The mass-produced process is very quick and the emphasis is mainly on how white the crumb is and how the product feels when you squeeze it.

A 'WHOLEGRAIN' OF TRUTH?

A report released in early 2013 by the UK's Real Bread Campaign investigated the marketing of industrially made loaves claiming to be 'wholegrain'. One loaf, from a leading supermarket chain, was found to contain just 6 per cent wholemeal flour as part of its ingredients list.

Real Bread Campaign's Chris Young said: 'What protection is there for shoppers? How can it be right that industrial loaf manufacturers are not prevented from tacking the word "wholegrain" to a loaf that could be 90-odd per cent white flour, or from stirring soya flour and highly refined gluten powder into a loaf whose name implies is made with 100 per cent wholemeal wheat flour?'

> Yes, it is possible to make your own affordable, healthy traditional bread as the ingredients for bread are simple, the most important one being time...

Ecologist: *Cynics might point to artisanal bread and write it off as another foodie trend. But does 'real' bread need to be expensive? Is it possible for ordinary people to buy or make their own, healthy, traditional bread?*

EH: […] In my book, *How to Make Bread*, I created every recipe in the book in a home oven, which shows that making artisanal bread can be done at home. Yes, it is possible to make your own affordable, healthy, traditional bread as the ingredients for bread are simple, the most important one being time …

Ecologist: *Lastly, what marks a good bread out from the rest, in terms of flavour and all round satisfaction?*

EH: A great bread is about the texture and taste. Use the best quality ingredients you can and take time in making your loaf. This is my advice. Bread is special. From the moment you start mixing the ingredients to the time when you take it out of the oven, tap it on the bottom to check for the hollow sound and then that unmistakeable smell that overwhelms you as the baked bread cools. It is magical!

WANT MORE INFO?
www.realbreadcampaign.org

LOSING OUT TO SUGAR

Sugar is almost universally popular – but recent years have seen some begin to question whether there is a hidden cost, to both people and the environment, attached to our love affair with this sweet wonder-food.

Trampling human rights

Sugar cultivation has been linked to a host of environmental problems, including deforestation, habitat loss, the use of pesticides and the pollution of land and water. Conditions for workers harvesting sugar or involved in processing it can also be poor, with low wages, substandard living conditions, and few health and safety procedures in place. Instances of forced labour have been reported, as has the use of child labour.

Journalist Sam Campbell investigated some of the allegations connected to sugar production – including claims that in Cambodia the livelihoods of poor farming communities were being devastated by the arrival of the crop. He reported for *The Ecologist* from Phnom Penh as part of our 'What's really in your cuppa?' special report:

Land grabbing

'We have documented widespread human rights abuses and environmental damage from all the major sugarcane

concessions, impacting more than 12,000 people in three provinces,' the head of one human rights organization said. 'The impact on local communities has been devastating. Families have been made landless and driven into

destitution and severe food insecurity. Hundreds have been made homeless and haven't received any compensation.'

The group published a report on the situation in 2010, claiming forced evictions, seizure and clearance of farmers' land and crops, destruction of forests, poisoning of local water resources and fisheries, arrests and harassment of human rights defenders, all connected to the sugar sector. Many Cambodians are farmers and rely on their smallholdings for survival.

Mostly poorly educated and often illiterate, villagers can be at the mercy of the authorities or powerful businessmen, especially if they have never legally registered their land with the central administration. Local officials reportedly in cahoots with land grabbers can betray those they are supposed to represent, tricking the most vulnerable out of their land and leaving them with nothing, campaigners claim.

Teng Kao, 48, says he lost 14.5 hectares he had occupied for 20 years to a sugar concession. He also claimed that residents' land had been recognized by local commune authorities, who issued documents. Instead of recognizing

villagers' ownership and compensating them, however, the widower and father of six claimed that villagers had been subjected to a campaign of intimidation, with cattle seized for ransom. He said two of his cows had been shot and killed.

'WE LOST EVERYTHING'

Cheav Ean, 64, is one of more than 200 families from three villages now living with the consequences of the nearby sugar cultivation. She claimed she had lived on her land since 1975, making it her legal property under Cambodian law. Nevertheless, she claims she lost 11.5 hectares to a sugar concession without any compensation.

'When the companies [...] arrived, we lost everything,' she said. '[...] We need to support five members of our family. ... I feel so depressed because I am getting older; I have no land; I don't know how to generate income to support our living; when I am sick, I don't have money for medication and our remaining land is so small that we cannot survive from farming it.'

WANT MORE INFO?
'What's Really in Your Cuppa?'
special report at
www.theecologist.org

THE HIDDEN COST OF PEPPER

5

> **...prices paid to farmers – per kg – were reduced to one fifth of what they had previously received in a matter of a few years.**

It's one of the most common kitchen staples, used to jazz up everything from casserole to curry to chips. But research by investigative outfit DanWatch found fluctuating market prices and poor harvests taking their toll on Indian pepper farmers struggling to make ends meet.

Suicides

The tropical state of Kerala in southern India is an increasingly popular destination for many European tourists, particularly those wanting to avoid the commercialism and overcrowding that now blight some of India's better known holiday spots such as Goa or Manali.

Kerala is also increasingly linked to Europe through its burgeoning export trade in black pepper. India as a whole is a major player in the global pepper supply chain, producing some 50,000 tonnes annually for both domestic and overseas markets – much of it sourced from Kerala's Wayanad region and a number of neighbouring districts.

But a disturbing report by the Danish organization DanWatch, published by *The Ecologist*, found that Kerala's pepper trade was linked to a wave of suicides among farmers, many struggling to make a living for themselves and their families following pepper price crashes in the 2000s.

Kerala's pepper crop is largely produced by small-scale farmers, each cultivating the spice on between 1 and 2 hectares of land. DanWatch claims that the prices paid to farmers – per kg – were reduced to one fifth of what they had previously received in a matter of a few years. At the same time, pepper yields declined because of a number of plant diseases.

The debt trap

According to the group, some 1,700 pepper farmers have killed themselves in Wayanad region during the past decade. They quote Dr Anil Kunar, from the agro-biodiversity centre MSSRF in Wayanad: 'The farmers could not repay their loans. Some took emergency loans to cover payments of existing loans, sometimes with an interest rate higher than 25 per cent. When a farmer could not repay, the bank or moneylender sent a letter of eviction. That letter was the crucial point where most of [those committing suicide] either hanged themselves or took poison by drinking their own pesticides.'

Aisha Schol, manager of Corporate Sustainability Analysis at Fairfood International, told DanWatch researchers: 'Smallscale pepper farmers are in a very vulnerable position. First and foremost, they have only pepper in their fields, so if pepper prices crash they […] lose everything. Secondly, the soil has seen an intensive use of chemicals from fertilizers and pesticides for decades. Diseases and crop failure are very common now. Again, they can lose everything.'

Although financial support from NGOs and the Kerala State Government has eased the situation, debt still remains widespread.

NEETHU'S STORY, AS TOLD TO DANWATCH

'One morning we awoke and found my dad having hanged himself in the bedroom, right here,' says 20-year-old Neethu, pointing towards a dark corner of a dusty bedroom. 'My mum and I knew we had financial difficulties. I knew that dad had taken a "blade loan" but I did not know how bad the situation was.'

A blade loan is a 'pay or die' loan from local moneylenders, often with exorbitant interest rates. Neethu assumes the moneylenders threatened her father to repay or hand over his land.

WANT MORE INFO?
www.danwatch.dk

6 Drinks

INTRODUCTION

Whether it's tea, coffee, fruit juices or fizzy pop, or even wine, beer or cider, there's probably something the ethical consumer needs to know about what they're drinking. *The Ecologist* has in recent years sought to unravel some of the hidden costs of our everyday drinks, and we've revealed some deeply unpleasant issues.

Did you know your tea could be linked to the sexual abuse of women at a supposedly ethically certified plantation supplying a leading brand? Or that the orange concentrates in your canned drink could have been picked by a worker earning poverty wages? Or that vineyard owners have been poisoned – including fatally – while producing wine?

These and other pieces have been compiled here, but we've also sought to highlight how some producers – including an international coffee company and an organic wine maker – are trying to mitigate their impacts on the environment and people.

THE HARD LABOUR BEHIND SOFT DRINKS

6

Low prices paid to Italian orange farmers supplying fruit for use in concentrates found in fizzy drinks are fuelling the use of migrant workers to harvest the annual crop – but conditions are appalling and exploitation is rife.

Scratching a living

It is perhaps the worst address in Western Europe. A ramshackle slum with a noisy road on one side, a railway on another and a stagnant-looking river flowing close by. The camp itself consists of little more than a collection of shoddily erected canvas tents and some abandoned buildings and sheds. Behind the wire fence, fires burn amid piles of rubbish – discarded wholesale-sized tins of olive oil, plastic bottles, newspapers, food scraps and other unidentifiable filth. Woodsmoke stings your eyes. As the winter sun falls, the scene is almost apocalyptic; dozens of migrants swarm around us – cooking, chopping firewood, calling out, trying to keep warm, their figures silhouetted against the flames.

They are from Africa – Ghana, Burkina Faso, Ivory Coast – and this squalid camp is currently home to at least two hundred itinerants. The migrants are here in Rosarno, in Calabria, southern Italy, to harvest the region's extensive orange crop. Each winter, as many as 2,000 migrants travel to this small agricultural town to scratch a living picking fruit that will end up on sale in markets and supermarkets, or as juices or concentrates used in the manufacture of soft drinks.

Many of the African migrants are in Italy illegally, having crossed the Mediterranean in often treacherous conditions in order to secure employment to send money back to their families. Most move between the major buildings or in makeshift slums on the edge of town. There's no electricity or running water. In many cases there's no functioning roof.

In the town's largest slum, some workers 'are forced to sleep outside, even in winter', according to Solomon, a migrant from Ghana who has been here for two months. 'Conditions are not good, as you can see,' he tells us, gesturing to the chaotic camp around us when we visit at night. Solomon says he has been in Italy itself for three years, in Naples before Rosarno, and came 'for economic, for financial reasons.'

Food parcels from local activists arrive while we are there – hot pasta from a local restaurant, some tinned food and other staples. One migrant agrees to distribute the provisions – not enough to go round for sure, but something.

When we return the following day, some of the migrants become unhappy at our presence – they say they are tired of journalists photographing them in this condition. One throws a stone. An angry confrontation begins, people gather around, there's shouting, in Italian, in French, in English. The situation is defused only by the intervention of our guide, and we agree to leave.

> **Many of the migrants ... live in appalling conditions, in run-down buildings or in makeshift slums on the edge of town.**

agricultural regions – Puglia, Campania, Sicily, Calabria and Basilicata – seeking piecework during the seasonal harvests of oranges, lemons, kiwis, olives, melons and tomatoes (see page 102).

Squalor & slums

Many of the migrants in Rosarno and the surrounding countryside live in appalling conditions, in run-down

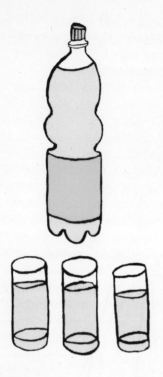

workers, so there is a paradox. At the end of the chain is a clash with poor people,' he says. The farmer sells his oranges to a local processing plant, which in turn sells to larger processing companies, which then process the fruit for large food and drink firms.

Unfair prices

Italy is a major producer of citrus fruits – around 3.6 million tonnes are cultivated from approximately 170,000 hectares of land. Calabria is the second biggest orange-growing area, producing more than 870,000 tonnes in 2009. The majority of the oranges grown around Rosarno are cheap, industrial-grade fruits favoured for processing into concentrates.

Italy's orange sector faces increasing competition from other producing countries including Brazil, China, the US, Mexico and Spain. According to Pietro Molinaro from Coldiretti Calabria, the regional branch of Italy's largest farmers' association, overseas competition combined with the low prices paid by large companies has resulted in orange growing becoming unviable for many farmers. They are – literally, he says – 'being squeezed'.

Poor returns

Migrants typically earn around 25 euros (£20) for a day's work, depending on the individual farmer, the market rate for oranges and whether a gangmaster makes deductions for transport or other 'services'. At one farm we visit that employs migrants, boss Alberto Callello maintains workers get a reasonable deal. '25 euros is the minimum wage, it is a poor wage but it is a poor economy. Poor but not exploitation,' he says.

Callello blames the economics of orange farming and the wider supply chain for the conditions. He says the market price has fallen below the cost of production: 'I get 7 cents per kilo for industrial oranges (used for concentrates) but need 8 cents per kilo to pay

Farmers themselves say this is why they are reliant on cheap, migrant labour: 'Young Italians are not likely to want to work in the fields... the only way is to use migrant workers because of the low wages connected to the harvest,' says Alberto Callello.

Coldiretti Calabria last year wrote to all the firms it says purchase orange ingredients from Calabria, highlighting what it believes are unfair prices paid for raw materials – a situation it says is fostering unpleasant conditions for workers. The group claims it never received a response.

WANT MORE INFO?
www.emergency.it

CONDITIONS WORSE THAN CONGO

The medical charity Emergency operates a twice-weekly mobile clinic in Rosarno – a specially converted coach with consultation and treatment rooms, as well as facilities for carrying out basic medical procedures.

'They [the patients] come in with muscle and skeletal conditions, respiratory problems, and may need specialist doctors such as a dentist,' says Dr Luca Corso. 'We have started to see [...] some cases that can be linked to working activities; mainly the improper use of pesticides and fungicides [...]. Mostly cases of irritative phenomena, for example, contact dermatitis in exposed areas such as hands and face, or conjuctivitis because the eyes are exposed.'

Angelo Moccia, the clinic's operations manager, says conditions here are worse than those he'd previously encountered in Congo. Andrea Freda, the clinic's nurse, adds: 'Conditions are not so different in Afghanistan to here.'

Although officially Italian hospitals are supposed to offer treatment to migrants, even those in the country illegally, there have been cases of workers being refused treatment, according to medical officials, with some migrants afraid to seek help because they fear being sent to internment camps.

BITTER HARVEST:
What links tea to the sexual abuse of women?

6

Tea is one of the world's most popular drinks. But it has been tainted by allegations of exploitation of some women working on tea estates in East Africa.

Rampant discrimination

'I can't show you my house,' Esther says, talking about her accommodation on a major tea plantation in East Africa. 'I'm just too embarrassed. I tried to get a transfer, but my options are a bribe of about 500 Kenya shillings [approximately £3.50] or to sleep with the supervisor. But he won't sleep with me. At 48 he thinks I am too old.'

Esther may not have slept with the supervisor on this occasion, but sexual abuse of women at this tea farm was found to be disturbingly common: sex was reportedly demanded by supervisors in return for allocating lighter duties, for help with securing better housing, organizing repairs to property or – in some cases – for extra money for women desperate to supplement their wages. Some women claimed they felt coerced into having intercourse in order to avoid being targeted by supervisors.

The tea farm involved is a flagship plantation of one of the world's biggest tea companies – producing instantly recognizable tea brands – stretching across more than 30,000 acres of land and employing 16,000 people. It's also endorsed by a leading ethical certification scheme. Problems were first highlighted by a Dutch research outfit who said they had uncovered 'rampant' discrimination and sexual harassment of women at the plantation, alongside other social problems. *The Ecologist* subsequently sent undercover reporter Verity Largo to investigate.

'I think of the money'

'It's completely normal here,' says Valerie. 'I'd say all of us, all the time,

" ...women pluckers who refuse the sexual advances of their, always male, supervisors are sometimes given too much work or allocated lonely or dangerous plucking zones.

sleep with the supervisor, or agree to have regular sex, in order to get a lighter shift.' According to Dutch researchers, 'women pluckers who refuse the sexual advances of their, always male, supervisors are sometimes given too much work or allocated lonely or dangerous plucking zones'.

Could this be regarded as prostitution? 'No, this isn't prostitution,' says Valerie. 'I didn't choose this. I have sex with supervisors to survive, to pay school fees, to keep my house or to get a repair done. I think of the money when I have sex, or what I am getting. Nothing else. There's no pleasure, or choice.'

A later report featured the story of Chanya. The single mother of two

claimed that, following an interview for a job at the plantation, a supervisor asked her for a bribe to secure employment. She informed the supervisor that she did not have the money. The supervisor then reportedly told her that to 'make her life easier' she should go to a house in the village to discuss the issue of her employment.

'[…] The supervisor told her that if she had sex with him he would guarantee that she got a job as a general worker, which was less strenuous than a tea picker. […] Chanya said she had no choice but to agree to the supervisor's advances because she had a child and dependents.'

HIV risk

'I grew up on that […] estate,' says another worker, Lavinia, 28. She lasted six months before she quit working at tea estates. She now has a different job. 'It is as bad as you see … sexual harassment and coercive sex [are] absolutely standard for all women under forty.'

Lavinia claims she watched both her sisters contract HIV. Both had been pressured into sex with tea supervisors, she says. 'I suppose the experience of watching my sister die in hospital [this was reportedly before anti-retrovirals were available] was just so deep,' she says. 'Then I found out my mum, who's also a tea picker [at the plantation], is positive. She's an old lady for god's sake. I just couldn't stay as a tea picker. I couldn't risk having unprotected sex just to keep my job.'

An 'issue of shame'

Why are the abuses not reported? The women said almost universally that they were fearful of losing their jobs, that the management couldn't be trusted to investigate properly and that the police were unlikely to take such claims seriously and would only take action in return for a bribe – which the women simply couldn't afford.

'I left. I complained, I went public, but no, I didn't report it. What would be the point? I'd have to pay the police to get my case heard… however bad it is. It's all they've got,' says Lavinia.

Arthur, a peer educator at the plantation, supports this view: 'I think the issue is one of shame; the women are encouraged to bear the shame and stigma… they find it almost impossible to insist on condoms. They don't report it because what would be the point?'

> **[she] claims she watched both her sisters contract HIV. Both had been pressured into sex with tea supervisors …**

The company behind the plantation initially denied the allegations, saying that working and living conditions at the estate were good and pointing towards the provision of schools, a hospital and health centres for workers and their families. It also highlighted that in order to retain certification from a leading ethical body it had to meet nearly 100 social, environmental and economic criteria. Audits by the certification body itself had found no evidence of problems, it maintained.

The company later acknowledged, however, that there appeared to be 'many problems to be resolved, at least at our own [...] plantation', and it is understood that efforts to tackle the problem have since been stepped up.

TEA: A VITAL SOURCE OF EMPLOYMENT

Tea is grown in more than 45 countries worldwide, and while India and China are the biggest producers, Sri Lanka and Kenya lead the way in exporting tea to meet global demand. Kenya's tea sector is a vital source of employment and income; in 2006, more than 300,000 tonnes was produced, creating an estimated 3 million jobs. According to the Kenyan Tea Board the country has, in recent years, been responsible for some 20 per cent of all the tea exported in the world. Much of the tea, after being picked, is put through a fermentation process, then dried, graded and processed. It then goes by road to large auctions in Mombasa. Typically, it is graded again, then blended, a process where tea from both large multinationals and small independent growers can be mixed together. Many large tea companies operate a system of vertical integration, controlling every stage of production.

CARBON COFFEE
Could drinking coffee help tackle the impacts of climate change?

6

A project funded by a leading Fairtrade coffee company is aiming to stop slash and burn farming in Peru by linking local reforestation to the international carbon market. But can such a scheme work, and will other companies follow suit?

Carbon trading

'We've tried to inspire others,' says Witney Kakos, Impact and Sustainability Manager at Cafédirect, talking about 'Reforestation Sierra Piura'. 'Companies know they need to invest in smallholder farmers down the supply chain.' The venture sees villagers in the remote Andes mountains paid to plant seedlings and manage tree nurseries. For every tonne of carbon 'captured' by the new trees, villagers receive one 'carbon credit'.

Credits are then sold on the international voluntary carbon market.

Although acknowledging that many companies have begun to invest in the emerging carbon offsetting market, Kakos says Cafédirect's approach is unique: 'We had to put in seed money [some £55,000 over six years for nearly 6,000 carbon credits], we paid upfront rather than just buy credits.'

As Matilda Lee reported for The Ecologist when she accompanied Cafédirect on a trip to the region in 2012, for each individual credit sold, 90 per cent of the revenue goes to fund further reforestation. The remaining 10 per cent funds climate adaptation projects for the coffee farmers down the mountain. The project appears to be having a positive impact.

CARBON CREDITS

Carbon credits are essentially permits that enable companies (or others) to emit a tonne of carbon dioxide (CO_2). The system was designed to help combat the growing threats of climate change. The money companies pay for credits is typically used to bankroll ethical initiatives, but credits can be directly traded for cash. Carbon trading has been criticized by some campaigners, with many schemes prone to failure or corruption.

Extreme weather

Thousands of smallholder coffee farmers [...] are learning how to adapt to extreme weather through [the project]. They are learning how to better manage shade trees and soil fertility on steep hillside farms [...]. But the farmers also came to realize that deforestation in a region 2,000 metres above them affects rainfall patterns and leaves them exposed to flash floods and soil erosion.

Subsistence farmers in the remote Choco village had over decades practised slash and burn agriculture to provide firewood and land to grow crops such as potatoes and corn for their families. The question was how to incentivize the people of Choco to manage their forests in the long term.

Longer term relief

'Simply donating the funds to plant trees might have provided short-term relief, but what would happen when those trees were needed for firewood or building?' asks Cafédirect's Head of Sustainability, Wolfgang Weinmann.

So far, over 224 hectares have been reforested; 70 per cent of the trees planted are pine and 30 per cent native quina. The community owns the land and reforesting it provides the villagers with an income and an incentive to sustainably manage the forest.

Kakos confirms the figures remain the same, and that the project is on track to achieve its targets, although there have been major challenges: 'It was difficult to get small landowners together... but we'd thought, how can smallholders be involved in this, there's big barriers to entry', she says. 'This is an example of [how] a marginalized sector of the population can benefit from ... the carbon market.'

WANT MORE INFO?
www.cafedirect.co.uk

WHAT'S REALLY IN YOUR CIDER?

6

Despite a boom in its popularity in recent years, are cider drinkers really aware of what they are consuming? Probably not, say a small band of cider experts who are doing their best to ensure people know the difference between a 'real' cider and a cheap, mass-produced, fizzy-apple-with-additives subsititute.

Exotic marketing

A renaissance in interest in cider has seen the big alcoholic companies and breweries spending a good deal of time and money marketing the 'stuff from apples'. It is now a prominent, must-have feature in many top restaurants, hip night clubs and supermarket booze aisles.

The current UK market in cider is estimated to be worth in excess of £860 million annually. This includes the fast-growing sub-sector of exotic fruit-flavoured ciders – mixed berry, strawberry, elderflower, lime and numerous other varieties – that have soared in popularity in the past few years, particularly among younger drinkers.

Although the UK is by far the biggest consumer of cider, South Africa, the US and Australasia are all developing their taste for the drink, say industry watchers, with recent years seeing sales jump. European countries traditionally associated with the drink, particularly France, have actually seen a decline in interest in cider.

Artificial ingredients

But some experts and fans of traditional 'real' cider – which they say should be made from apples and pretty much apples alone – are increasingly critical of mass-produced cider drinks and question whether consumers are getting a good deal. They also invite scrutiny of the ingredients and processes that lie behind some of these drinks:

'Instead of being made from all juice as a true cider would be, they're made with a little bit of apple juice and a bunch of sugar-water. Mass-produced cider sold in the UK is mostly made from imported apple concentrate; artificial colourings, sweeteners, and preservatives are added to make up for the apple character that isn't there. The liquid is then filtered, pasteurized to kill the yeast, and kept and served under carbon dioxide pressure,' leading cider watcher – and blogger – Jim Callender writes.

He argues that 'real cider' is made simply by fermenting the juice of apples 'with nothing added and nothing taken away'. He also believes cider is a drink that has not been 'pasteurized, carbonated, or concentrated' and uses only 'locally sourced apples, pressed and fermented using traditional cider production methods …'

Bland taste

Middle Farm, in East Sussex, is home to the national collection of cider and perry. The farm holds over 100 draft cider and perry varieties and 200 bottled products, many made by independent, artisanal producers. The farm does much to champion the traditional art of cider making and highlight its cultural importance.

Rod Marsh, who runs the collection, which started in earnest in 1993, agrees that some of the mass-produced drinks available in pubs or off licences aren't really ciders at all. But he also says –

perhaps conversely – that the huge growth in their popularity is having a positive impact on traditional producers: 'Artisanal growers are benefiting from [these] bland products, that side is burgeoning… trade sales have gone through the roof,' he says. 'People are getting bored with the mass-produced drinks.'

With the industrial production processes involved in making many populist ciders 'you lose the goodness of the apple,' Marsh continues, before stating that you 'can't commodify something that has 2,000 years of history.'

WANT MORE INFO?
www.real-cider.co.uk
www.middlefarm.com

WHAT'S REALLY IN YOUR WINE?

6

Studies have found that many conventionally produced wines contain levels of pesticides that should ring the alarm bells. But one pioneering wine producer has trailblazed a path that offers an alternative – protecting the land and reducing the risk to consumers.

Health risk

Wine production globally involves the use of significant quantities of pesticides, and in 2011 Yannick Chenet, a 43-year-old French farmer, had the unfortunate accolade of becoming the first winegrower whose death was linked to pesticide use. The case attracted little attention outside of France, but jolted the country's sizeable and influential wine industry into at least acknowledging a problem with pesticides.

However, a study published early in 2013 by Excell Laboratories, based in Bordeaux, found that nine out of ten sampled French wines still contained traces of pesticides. Although the levels found were under the limits judged as safe by the French authorities, some wines tested saw as many as nine separate pesticide residues present.

Earlier studies had found similar cases. Pesticide Action Network Europe, working in conjunction with Greenpeace Germany and others, revealed in 2008 how it had purchased 40 bottles of wine, both conventional and organic, across the EU, and sent them for testing. Every single conventionally produced wine was found to contain pesticides – on average four different chemicals per bottle – and many were found to contain pesticides classed as carcinogens or endocrine disruptors.

The researchers claimed that had the levels been judged against European drinking water standards, none of the conventional wines would have passed strict human consumption criteria. Staggeringly, according to those behind the report, 'on average, pesticides were present [in sampled wine] at levels 230 times higher than legally permitted in drinking water'. No pesticide traces were found in the – five – organic wines sampled.

Outlawing chemicals

Near the historic town of Battle in East Sussex, Roy Cook and his wife Irma have chosen to do things differently. The pair own and run Sedlescombe, England's oldest and biggest organic vineyard.

'I'm concerned about what has gone into my food and wine,' says Roy. 'The risks of [pesticide] spraying bring it home.' The Sedlescombe vineyard is run to strict organic – and now biodynamic – principles, which outlaw the use of pesticides, herbicides or other artificial inputs and seek to enhance the land through environmentally friendly cultivation techniques.

Enhancing nature

'[Our approach] is completely opposite to conventional chemical farming where they seek to dominate nature,' says Roy. 'We [attempt to] maximize the fertility of soil, land and the quality of the grapes. I don't think the chemical approach is sustainable in the long term.'

The vineyard, established in 1979, produced its first certified-organic wine in 1982. Back then, even attempting to grow grapes in the UK was seen as adventurous, let alone trying to do so organically. 'There was scepticism initially as we were trying to do these two impossible things,' says Roy. 'Generally [now], people have a lot of respect for you, the quality is top notch.'

Sedlescombe is now a significant and highly respected supplier of eco-friendly wines producing up to 30,000 bottles of wine – red, white and sparkling – a year. The weather in some recent years – 2012 particularly – took its toll, with the vineyard managing only 3,000 bottles, but the outfit supplements its income by offering farm tours, wine tastings, lunches and other tourist activities.

WANT MORE INFO?
www.panna.org
www.englishorganicwine.co.uk

Sources & References

FRUIT

How fair are organic & Fairtrade bananas?

Unpeeling the banana trade,
FAIRTRADE FOUNDATION,
www.fairtrade.org.uk

How fair are organic and Fairtrade bananas?,
THE ECOLOGIST www.theecologist.org

The deadly legacy of Guatemala's banana trade

(GUATEMALA) SOLIDARITY CENTER,
www.solidaritycenter.org

Another banana union rep killed,
US LABOR EDUCATION IN THE AMERICAS
PROJECT, www.usleap.org

Take action to end the killing in Guatemala,
BANANALINK, www.bananalink.org.uk

Cleaning up the pineapple chain

Why pineapples matter,
BANANALINK,
www.bananalink.org.uk

Bitter fruit: the truth about supermarket pineapple,
THE GUARDIAN, www.theguardian.com

A tale of two apple farms

H. E. HALL & SON, www.hehall.co.uk

SOIL ASSOCIATION, www.soilassociation.org

ENGLAND IN PARTICULAR,
Orchards, trees and orchard products,
www.england-in-particular.info

The Peruvian mango trade

*Peruvian mango production: not enough
improvements,*
OXFAM GERMANY, SOMO, www.somo.nl

Fancy a mango? Think twice ...
THE ECOLOGIST, www.theecologist.org

Ethical fruit: what are the alternatives?

ETHICAL FRUIT COMPANY,
www.ethicalfruitcompany.co.uk

VEGETABLES

**Hard labour: the invisible workforce toiling in
our salad fields**

*Bitter harvest: how exploitation and abuse stalks
migrant workers on UK farms,*
THE ECOLOGIST, www.theecologist.org

GANGMASTERS LICENSING AUTHORITY,
www.gla.defra.gov.uk

*Experiences of forced labour in the UK
food industry,*
JOSEPH ROWNTREE FOUNDATION,
www.jrf.org.ukg

Ghosts, the film, www.nickbroomfield.com

Inside a salad 'mega farm'

*Inside the salad 'mega farm' supplying the UK's
appetite for lettuce,*
THE ECOLOGIST, www.theecologist.org

Chemical warfare: what's really in our veg?

PESTICIDE ACTION NETWORK UK,
www.pan-uk.org

Magic mushrooms

MAESYFFIN MUSHROOMS,
www.maesymush.co.uk

**Grow! The young farmers standing up
to 'Big Ag'**

Grow!, the film, www.growmovie.net

GREENHORNS, to promote, recruit and support
new farmers in America,
www.thegreenhorns.net

Could horsepower be the future of farming?

CHAGFORD COMMUNITY MARKET GARDEN,
www.chagfood.org.uk

*The new breed of young farmer:
Ed Hamer, Dartmoor,*
THE OBSERVER, www.theguardian.comk

THE LAND WORKERS' ALLIANCE,
www.landworkersalliance.org.uk

MEAT & FISH
Inside an industrial pig factory

Farms not factories, PIG BUSINESS,
www.pigbusiness.co.uk

'Shocking' farms raise pigs for UK,
THE OBSERVER, www.theguardian.com

The game meat hoax

*The economic and environmental impact of
sporting shooting*,
BASC, www.shootingfacts.co.uk

The UK game bird industry, a short study,
DEFRA / ADAS, www.archive.defra.gov.uk

*Government welfare body attacks 'gamebird'
battery cages*,
ANIMAL AID, www.animalaid.org.uk

Gunsmoke and Mirrors, the film,
www.youtube.com

*Cramped, filthy and featherless – the 'battery'
game birds sold as delicacy*,
THE GUARDIAN, www.theguardian.com

Soy wars

Fix the food chain,
FRIENDS OF THE EARTH, www.foe.co.uk

Killing fields: the true cost of Europe's cheap meat,
THE ECOLOGIST, www.theecologist.org

The hidden cost of salmon

*How our growing appetite for salmon is
devastating coastal communities in Peru*,
THE ECOLOGIST, www.theecologist.org

THE PURE SALMON CAMPAIGN,
www.puresalmon.org

Blood fish: the real cost of prawn curry

*Why prawns should be blacklisted from all our
shopping baskets*,
THE ECOLOGIST, www.theecologist.org

Putting the real price of shrimp on the agenda,
ENVIRONMENTAL JUSTICE FOUNDATION,
www.ejfoundation.org/shrimp

Fishy business: the illegal shellfish trade that threatens our health

*Revealed: the illegal shellfish trade that's putting
consumer health at risk*,
THE ECOLOGIST, www.theecologist.org

DAIRY
Just how healthy is soya milk?

Behind the label: soya,
THE ECOLOGIST, www.theecologist.org

They hailed it as a wonderfood,
THE OBSERVER, www.theguardian.com

The truth about goat's milk

British goat farms exposed
VIVA!, www.viva.org.uk

Sour milk: inside the US 'mega-dairy' industry

NOT IN MY CUPPA, www.wspa.org.uk

*Sour milk: undercover inside the US'
super dairy' industry*,
ECOLOGIST FILM UNIT,
www.ecologistfilmunit.com

What's really in your cuppa?,
THE ECOLOGIST, www.theecologist.org

Biodynamic cows: the micro-dairy challenging conventional milk production

TABLEHURST AND PLAW HATCH
COMMUNITY FARM,
www.tablehurstandplawhatch.co.uk

BIODYNAMIC ASSOCIATION,
www.biodynamic.org.uk

Muck and magic,
THE ECOLOGIST, www.theecologist.org

GROCERY
Tainted tomatoes

*Scandal of the 'tomato slaves' harvesting crop
exported to UK*,
THE ECOLOGIST, www.theecologist.org

OSSERVATORIO MIGRANTI BASILICATA,
www.osservatoriomigrantibasilicata.it

Drizzle with care

Tom Mueller, *Extra Virginity: The Sublime
and Scandalous World of Olive Oil*
NEW YORK: W. W. NORTON, 2012

The green gold rush,
IRPI, www.irpi.eu

Drizzle with care,
THE ECOLOGIST, www.theecologist.org

Bad eggs: why there's something rotten down on the farm

Cracked, VIVA!, www.viva.org.uk

Real bread

Emmanuel Hadjiandreou, *How to Make Bread*
LONDON: RYLAND PETERS & SMALL, 2011.

REAL BREAD CAMPAIGN,
www.sustainweb.org/realbread/

Losing out to sugar

*Revealed: the bitter taste of Cambodia's
sugar boom*,
THE ECOLOGIST, www.theecologist.org

What's really in your cuppa?,
THE ECOLOGIST, www.theecologist.org

The hidden cost of pepper

DANWATCH, www.danwatch.dk

The hidden cost of pepper,
THE ECOLOGIST, www.theecologist.org

Spices: the true cost of a kitchen staple,
THE ECOLOGIST, www.theecologist.org

DRINK
The hard labour behind soft drinks

*Coca Cola challenged over orange harvest linked
to "exploitation and squalor'*,
THE ECOLOGIST, www.theecologist.org

COLDIRETTI, www.coldiretti.it

Bitter harvest: what links tea to the sexual abuse of women?

*PG Tips and Lipton tea hit by 'sexual
harassment and poor conditions' claims*,
THE ECOLOGIST, www.theecologist.org

SOMO, www.somo.nl/themes-en/tea

Carbon coffee: could drinking coffee help tackle the impacts of climate change?

*Coffee farmers in Peru look to carbon market
to find climate adaptation*,
THE ECOLOGIST, www.theecologist.org

*Keeping our daily coffee: the farmers in Peru
adapting to climate change*,
THE ECOLOGIST, www.theecologist.org

What's really in your cider?

Real Cider blog, www.real-cider.co.uk

National Collection of Cider and Perry,
MIDDLE FARM, www.middlefarm.com

What's really in your wine?

SEDLESCOMBE ORGANIC VINEYARD,
www.englishorganicwine.co.uk

Message in a bottle,
PESTICIDE ACTION NETWORK, www.pan-europe.
info/Resources/Briefings/Message_in_a_Bottle.pdf

French winegrowers warned over pesticides,
THE TELEGRAPH, www.telegraph.co.uk

Further Reading

www.ecologistguidetofood.com

Barry Estabrook, *Tomatoland*,
MISSOURI: ANDREWS MCMEEL, 2011

Seth Holmes, *Fresh Fruit, Broken Bodies*,
CALIFORNIA: UNIVERSITY OF
CALIFORNIA PRESS, 2013

Margaret Gray,
*Labour and the Locavore: The Making
of a Comprehensive Food Ethic*,
CALIFORNIA: UNIVERSITY OF
CALIFORNIA PRESS, 2011

Felicity Lawrence,
*Not on the Label: What Really Goes into
the Food on your Plate*,
LONDON: PENGUIN, 2004

Joanna Blythman,
*Shopped: The Shocking Power
of British Supermarkets*,
LONDON: FOURTH ESTATE, 2004

Hsiao-Hung Pai, *Chinese Whispers:
The True Story Behind Britain's Hidden
Army of Labour*,
LONDON: PENGUIN, 2008

Dan Imhoff, *CAFO: The Tragedy
of Industrial Animal Factories*,
CALIFORNIA: WATERSHED MEDIA, 2010

Wenonah Hauter, *Foodopoly:
The Battle Over the Future of Food
and Farming in America*,
NEW YORK: THE NEW PRESS, 2012

Saru Jayaraman,
Behind the Kitchen Door,
NEW YORK: CORNELL UNIVERSITY
PRESS, 2012

Gabriel Thompson, *Working in the
Shadows: A Year of Doing the Jobs (Most)
Americans Don't Want to Do*,
NEW YORK: NATION BOOKS, 2010

About *The Ecologist*

**The Ecologist is the world's leading
environmental affairs title and has been
setting the environmental agenda for over
40 years – bringing the critical issues of our
time into the mainstream through cutting-
edge reporting, as well as pioneering
original thinking and inspiring action.**

Founded in 1970 by Edward Goldsmith, the
magazine shot to fame in 1972 for devoting an
entire issue to its Blueprint for Survival, a radical
manifesto for change that proposed, amongst
other reforms, the formation of a movement for
survival. This led to the creation of the People
Party, later renamed the Ecology Party and finally
the Green Party.

In the years that followed, the magazine continued
to break new ground in the environmental debate,
notably by pointing to global climate change
during the African droughts of the mid-1970s, and
exposing the extent of the slash-and-burn
operations ravaging the Amazon rainforest during
the early 1980s. It went on to unveil the fallacy of
plentiful nuclear energy during the era in which
the technology's future was thought to herald
electricity 'too cheap to meter'.

During the last ten years, *The Ecologist* has
continued to highlight the contradictions of
economic globalization, the health effects of
everyday toxins, and the huge environmental
cost of industrial agriculture. Its continued
coverage has pushed many of these issues
into the mainstream.

The Ecologist aims to encourage its readers to
challenge conventional thinking and tackle global
issues at a local level. In 2012, *The Ecologist*
merged with *Resurgence* magazine, creating a
stronger voice for the environmental movement
to inform and inspire change.

Index